THE UPSET BOOK

HOW TO DEAL
WITH UPSET PEOPLE

Second Edition
Revised and Expanded

Pennie Myers & Don Nance

D1457051

MAC PRESS

The Upset Book
is published by
MAC PRESS
14301 Brookline Court
Wichita, Kansas 67230
(316) 689-4225

**Library of Congress Cataloging in
Publication Data**

© 1986, 1991 by Pennie Myers, Ed.D. and Don Nance, Ph.D.
All rights reserved including the right of reproduction
in whole or in part in any form.

ISBN 0-9620723-5-4

CONTENTS

Acknowledgments

About the Authors

Acknowledgments

A special thank you to our clients, workshop participants, friends and family members who, through the years, have shared many of their personal experiences with us. It is to all of them that this book is dedicated.

CHAPTER ONE
SIX PRINCIPLES FOR
DEALING WITH UPSET PEOPLE

ONE

The woman who entered our office looked
considerably older than thirty-five, the age
which appeared on her client file. She sank into
a chair and announced that she wasn't sure
whether she needed work-related consultation
or marital counseling. Peggy was the customer
service representative for a large utility
company. Most of her day was spent coping
with upset consumers. She was exhausted by
her daily contact with angry people who had
gripes against the company. Many of her work
days ended unhappily. Either she inappropriately exploded at a customer or she stalked
home and played "kick the dog" with members
of her family — sometimes both. Peggy was
fearful of losing her job. She worried about her
relationship with her family. A friend of Peggy's
suggested she call us for some help dealing with
upset people. Improving her people skills, she
hoped, would also improve her job and her
family situation.

Peggy's problem is a problem for all of us. No one
escapes dealing with upset people. No one escapes
feeling upset. Upset people are people whose irritation,
anger, sadness or grief has been activated. Friends,
family members, customers and colleagues in the
workplace are sometimes upset people. Nice people,
quiet people, easy-going people, slow to anger people all
experience feelings of upset at times. Each of us has been

both an upset person and the one who has had to deal with others who are upset.

This book presents a systematic plan for dealing with upset people. We anticipate that when you finish the book you'll be able to make three statements about yourself when it comes to dealing with upset people:

> "I already have some of the attitudes and behaviors that help in dealing with upset people." (Each of us has already acquired many skills related to dealing with people who are upset. We hope you will take time to praise and appreciate your skills.)

"I learned some new ways to prevent and handle upset in others." (We can only do what we know how to do. The more behaviors we know how to use, the more opportunity we have to succeed. New skills are developed through learning and practicing.)

> "I have learned some new ways of thinking about, organizing and using principles related to upset people." (Understanding what causes upset, understanding what happens to *us* when we are confronted with an upset person and understanding why some strategies work better than others when dealing with upset people improves our chances for success when it comes to dealing with upset people.)

As you read this book, think about the upset people you've had to deal with and imagine yourself replaying some of the scenes with the attitudes and behaviors described. Each of us knows at least one or two people who are going to remain upset no matter what we say or do. Nothing could help to reduce their upset. These people are atypical and in the minority. Allow yourself to focus on the majority of people with whom the principles for dealing with upset people outlined in this book will work.

The Upset Book is rooted in the belief that much of the upset that we encounter can be prevented by utilizing positive contact skills with people. Therefore, our book addresses how to prevent upset in people who initially are not upset at all. Of course, in addition to "prevention" skills, we also need "curative" skills for people who are already upset. Our formulas for dealing with complaints, anger, grief and other difficult situations grew and developed in the fertile soil of several well-accepted theories and found fruition in the basics of good communication.

The chapters in *The Upset Book* are organized in the following way. Chapter Two describes the seven channels of communication. These channels of communication will serve as our communication building blocks for dealing with upset people. Chapter Three presents several basic ideas from Transactional Analysis. These ideas help to explain some of the causes of upset. They also help us to understand which strategies are most likely to succeed in dealing with upset in others. Chapter Four focuses on how to manage our *own* upset when dealing with others who are upset. Preventing upset is the subject of Chapter Five. When we successfully prevent upset, we have fewer upset people to handle. Chapter Six is about complaints — what they are and what they mean. Chapter Seven provides a formula for handling upset people and addresses some common problems encountered in dealing with upset in others. How to handle angry people is the subject of Chapter Eight. This chapter discusses the causes of anger and includes a formula for handling angry people as well as specific techniques for defusing extreme anger. Chapter Nine describes methods for dealing with people who have experienced loss, grief or some difficult change in their lives. Upset can be the result of many kinds of loss including the death of a loved one, loss of a job, loss of possessions, divorce, children leaving home to start their adult lives, the loss of health or the aging process. The final chapter summarizes the basic premises of the book and focuses on how to put the concepts discussed in the book into practice.

Within some of the following chapters are skill-building activities related to the discussion in that particular chapter. The way to improve at something is through practice. Athletes know this and spend many hours perfecting their skills in practice rather than attempting to develop their skills at the game. We hope you will consider the activities within various sections of the book as opportunities for practice and use them as suggested activities from which you can create additional ways for handling upset people. Also, please keep in mind that once the basics of a new skill are learned, we must go out in the field to gain experience. Don't expect to perform flawlessly. Expect only improved performance over time. Don't be afraid to use what you are learning and don't be too hard on yourself.

Before reading any further, take a few minutes to complete the Dealing with Upset People Profile. By completing this profile, you will be able to identify some of the attitudes and behaviors that contribute to the upset of other people. The profile may also help you to understand what it is that upsets *you* when you are faced with a complaining, angry or depressed person. Some of the principles for dealing with upset people that we will be discussing throughout the book are previewed in the profile. You may find it helpful to relate specific situations that you have encountered to each of the questions. Our hope is that the profile will get you into the mood for mastering the art of dealing with people who are upset. In Chapter Eight, we will review the profile and discuss each of the statements in it.

Dealing With Upset People Profile

Please rate each of the following twelve statements by assigning it the number on the five-point scale that most closely matches how you see yourself.

almost never	infre- quently	some- times	usually	almost always
5	4	3	2	1

1) ___ I have trouble listening to people because there are no new complaints — just the same old ones replayed over and over again.

2) ___ I am afraid to show concern for other people's problems for fear these people will expect me to do something about their problems.

3) ___ My day is made or ruined by the moods of people around me.

4) ___ I try to convince other people by talking a lot and using logical arguments.

5) ___ I talk about myself a lot.

6) ___ I hate to be interrupted by people when I'm in the middle of working on something.

7) ___ I am uncomfortable when I don't know the answer to a question I am asked or when I don't know what to say to an upset person.

8) ___ I have trouble listening to people's problem if I know I won't be able to find a solution to their problems.

9) ___ I feel that other people's upset is personally directed at me.

10) ___ I feel that it is important for me to talk rationally at all times when dealing with an upset person.

11) ___ I don't like to refer upset people to others who might be helpful to them because it says I am not being helpful enough.

12) ___ I feel frustrated when I don't have the power to help people resolve their problems.

___ TOTAL SCORE

Add your individual item scores for a total score. Your score can range from 12 to 60. The higher your score, the more successful you are likely to be at handling upset people. Scores above 42 suggest above-average attitudes and skills related to handling people. If you score below 36, you probably need to improve some of your attitudes and behaviors in order to deal successfully with people. We hope that by the time you have read *The Upset Book* and practiced the behaviors outlined throughout it, your Dealing with Upset People Profile score will be at an above-average level and you will feel more comfortable about handling upset situations. We recommend retaking the profile for self-assessment purposes after you have finished the book.

Six Principles For Dealing With Upset People

Self-Esteem

Six principles form the foundation for handling upset people. The first principle is: **It is important to interact with others in such a way that no-one's self-esteem is damaged.** In dealing with upset people, we can become upset by our own behavior as well as by the behavior of the upset person. This is most likely to happen if we have behaved inappropriately — perhaps yelling back or not being as helpful as we might have been. The goal in handling others who are upset is to have all of the participants in the situation feel good about the way in which they conducted themselves. Everyone should be able to feel proud of his or her own behavior. No one should need to avoid further contact due to anger or embarrassment.

> Not long ago, after presenting this material to the sales force of a large midwestern manufacturing company, one of the employees described someone with whom she had had many upsetting phone conversations. She felt hopeless about ever developing a satisfactory business relationship with this person. After attending our Dealing with Upset People Seminar, she reluctantly decided to give some of the "stuff" a try. To her surprise, things improved. Her job became more pleasant and she felt good about her ability to cope with a difficult person.

It helps when, at the end of the day, you feel you handled

yourself and others well. This reduces the probability of catching and spreading the "upset person syndrome." Being irritable at the end of a difficult work day is unlikely to improve the situation. We only spread our upset to our loved ones.

The Most Important Person

Do you have a favorite store? What about the business establishment with which you vowed never again to do business? Is there a friend with whom you consistently enjoy spending time? Are your preferences about where to trade, shop and eat based on particular people? If so, you readily can get a sense of the second principle for dealing with upset people. The second principle is: **The most important person in any setting is the contact person.** The impact of the contact person is immediate. Customers, clients or patients are as frequently won or lost by receptionists, salespeople and service representatives as they are by management policies, products or professionals. I (Pennie) value good medical care. I liked my doctor and respected her competence. However, I changed family physicians based on frequent difficulties with the physician's receptionist. I (Don) enjoy weekend breakfasts at a particular restaurant because one of the waiters is so pleasant and competent — not because the eggs are noticeably superior.

The principle of the "most important person" means that each of us has the power to affect the well-being of those around us. Our impact is strong and immediate. In our work settings and as parents, spouses, friends and lovers, we are more important than we sometimes feel.

Being in Charge of Yourself

A third principle for dealing with upset people is:
People can be in charge of their own behavior in ways that help them successfully manage the behavior of others. The only person whose behavior we can control is our own. By staying in charge of ourselves we *can* have an impact on what happens in our dealings with other people. If we approach other people with a smile, they smile back because they expect to have a pleasant interaction with us. On the other hand, if we approach others with an angry facial expression or clenched fists, they prepare themselves for self-protection. How we approach other people influences how they respond to us. It is possible through self-mastery to have mostly positive relationships with other people. We can use our own behavior to elicit the behaviors we want from other people.

> A discouraged repairman, in talking about his customers, said: "If they're nice to me, I'm nice to them and if they're not nice to me, I'm not nice to them." "Do you mean that even if you've been driving down the road singing and feeling great, a growling customer can change your entire mood and make you feel lousy," we asked. "Yup," he replied.

How powerless people permit themselves to be when they allow others to control their moods so easily! Being in charge of yourself encourages the successful handling of upset people.

Fighting the Natural Tendencies

Closely related to the principle of being in charge of yourself is the fourth principle for dealing with upset people which is: **Effective dealing with upset people requires us to fight our natural tendencies.** Almost every natural response to an upset person is ineffective in reducing the upset. For example, the natural tendency when approached by an angry person is to be angry in return. Yet, angry people who complain about the way in which we treated them are likely to escalate their anger if we get angry in return. Similarly, we must fight our natural tendency to avoid upset. If one is already upset, then being ignored only adds fuel to the fire. The instinctive response to being blamed is to defend or blame in return. Like other natural tendencies, defending or blaming in return increases rather than reduces upset. Fighting natural tendencies is no easy task! But, it *is* possible to learn to control instinctive behavior in favor of self-control. The ideas and suggestions throughout this book are aimed at helping the reader to control natural tendencies that are ineffective in handling upset people. This is hard work, yet the benefits are great!

Primary and Secondary Upset

The fifth principle in dealing with upset people is: **Primary upset needs to be managed so that it will not escalate into secondary upset.** Secondary upset is the upset that results from not having our initial upset or complaint handled appropriately. A consumer story illustrates the principle of primary versus secondary upset.

When my (Pennie's) daughter was three years old her grandmother bought her a bathrobe for her birthday. Grandmother thought she'd purchased a size four. When the box was opened, the robe was a size six. A hurried trip was made to exchange the robe for the correct size.At that point grandmother, mother and daughter had primary upset — a touch of annoyance at having to exchange the gift. After dealing with the salesperson, the primary upset escalated into secondary upset. We became disturbed and upset by the way in which we were treated. The salesperson noticed a missing button on the robe. She said, "I think you are returning used merchandise." Her accusations escalated and our upset increased. She refused to exchange the robe. Suffice it to say that in the last twenty-five years no-one in our family has purchased anything from this particular children's store. The salesperson cost the store dearly by her poor handling of a simple complaint.

Simple complaints are not responsible for divorces or severed business relationships. Poorly handled complaints are! Lost sales or impaired relationships are expensive to the parties involved. The good news is that while secondary upset is costly, it is also almost always preventable. While we may not have been able to prevent someone's primary upset, we can almost always stay in charge of ourselves in such a way as to insure that the primary upset does not escalate into secondary upset. The importance of preventing secondary upset cannot be overemphasized.

Soft to Hard

The last principle in dealing with upset people is: **Working from soft to hard**. Working from soft to hard means that we use the softest behaviors possible in dealing with other people. Security guards and police dogs are unnecessary when an understanding ear will do as well or better. An admonishing look may be all that is necessary to quiet a noisy child. "I'm sorry you had a bad day" has helped calm many an upset spouse or friend. Kind, courteous and quick responses help to reduce most people's upset. Save your strongest measures for those situations that require more drastic strategies. It makes more sense to move from soft to hard than to start out hard and have no place to go. Children of parents who yell all the time simply have learned to turn down their parents' volume. When our toddler runs out into the street, we want to reprimand sternly and in a no-nonsense manner. If it takes an angry voice to let the child know how serious we are, then that is what we do. But the toddler who needs a reminder to pick up his or her toys at the end of the day doesn't need the first reminder to involve raised voices. The most successful parents, like the most successful managers, are those who match the level of their involvement to the situation. Working soft to hard saves everyone unnecessary wear and tear.

By now you have completed your Dealing With Upset People Profile and have an understanding of the principles involved in handling people who are upset. It is time to turn our attention to the building blocks that prepare us to deal with upset people.

■

CHAPTER TWO
SEVEN CHANNELS
OF COMMUNICATION

TWO

In a voice that suggested countless repetitions of the same question, the woman behind the chest-high counter at the travel club asked, "How can I help you?" We requested several local maps and a tour guide book for the area. She gathered the requested materials mumbling and grumbling to herself. She handed us the tour book and announced in an irritated tone, "You should get tour books at your local chapter office." Then she filled out a club exchange receipt and presented it mechanically for a signature. The message she was communicating came through loud and clear and bore little resemblance to her initial suggestion of wanting to be helpful.

Good communication is important for preventing and managing upset in people. The purpose of this chapter is to describe the basic components of communication. These components will be used as building blocks in the formulas described in subsequent chapters. We need a common frame of reference for understanding what is happening in the communication process. The channels of communication described in this chapter are useful for understanding communication at a *behavioral* level. We will look at a model for understanding communicating with upset people at a *psychological* level in Chapter Three.

The Communication Process

Every time we engage in even the briefest interaction with someone, a very complex process of communication is taking place. We are so accustomed to this process, that usually we are totally unaware of its complexity. Communicating is like driving an automobile. After we have been driving a while, we stop paying attention to the individual tasks of accelerating, breaking, changing gears, steering and so forth. If, however, we suddenly became accident prone after years of driving, it would be essential to analyze each element of our driving. Similarly, if we are having problems dealing with upset people, we need to look carefully at the communication process to see what needs correcting.

We are called upon countless times every day to use our own channels of communication in sending messages and to attend to other people's channels of communication in order to decipher the messages sent to us. Good communicators send the same message on all channels. Good communicators are also skilled at scanning the senders' channels of communication.

The following self-assessment tool has no right or wrong answers. You need only assess yourself as to current skill level on a number of communication dimensions. The Communication Questionnaire can also be a useful tool for asking other people to evaluate your communication skills. It can be helpful to ask a boss, supervisee, friend or family member to fill out the questionnaire about you.

Interpersonal Communication Inventory

Please rate yourself by placing a check mark in the column which most fits your assessment of your current behavior on each item.

	Doing Well	Doing All Right	Need To Do Less	Need to Do More
Being concise and getting to the point	___	___	___	___
Being forceful and definite rather than hesitant and apologetic	___	___	___	___
Being specific and giving examples in order to make communication more clear	___	___	___	___
Giving an overview when details are not necessary	___	___	___	___
Letting others know when I do not understand something they have said	___	___	___	___
Letting others know when I like something they have said or done	___	___	___	___
Letting others know when I disagree with them	___	___	___	___
Letting others know when I think they have strayed from the topical conversation	___	___	___	___
Letting others know when I am getting irritated or angry	___	___	___	___

Letting others know when
I feel hurt by something
they have said or done   ___   ___   ___   ___

Listening to understand
rather than preparing my
next remark   ___   ___   ___   ___

Helping others participate
in a conversation or in a
discussion   ___   ___   ___   ___

Checking to make sure I
understand what others
are saying   ___   ___   ___   ___

Summarizing points of
agreement and
disagreement   ___   ___   ___   ___

Asking questions
that get information   ___   ___   ___   ___

Checking out with others
what I think they are feeling   ___   ___   ___   ___

Attending to the feelings
of an upset person   ___   ___   ___   ___

Responding to a person
who is expressing
closeness   ___   ___   ___   ___

Talking in group
discussions   ___   ___   ___   ___

Being aware when I am
coping with my own
feelings   ___   ___   ___   ___

Getting feedback
from others   ___   ___   ___   ___

Being able to stand silence   _____   _____   _____   _____

Being able to stand conflict   _____   _____   _____   _____

Accepting help from others   _____   _____   _____   _____

Offering help to others   _____   _____   _____   _____

Giving in to others   _____   _____   _____   _____

Asserting myself   _____   _____   _____   _____

Backing up others when
necessary   _____   _____   _____   _____

Once you (and perhaps others) have completed the Communication Questionnaire, select three items that you or others think you do well. Enjoy feeling good about these skills. Also select three items on which you would like to improve. As you continue reading the book, utilize the skill-building exercises in order to improve in the targeted areas.

Seven Channels of Communication

Anytime people are communicating, they are doing so in many different ways. We are labeling the different methods by which people communicate the *channels of communication*. These seven channels are the building blocks of communication.

Channel One: Language

The first channel of communication is the language channel. The "what" of our message is transmitted on this channel through the words we choose and the way we string them together. It stands to reason that if two people speak different languages, it can be difficult, perhaps impossible, for them to communicate. Yet, even within languages, miscommunication easily occurs when words have different meanings to different people. The travel club woman described at the beginning of this chapter said, "How can I help you?" Those words were translated literally by the traveler while apparently meaning, "I hope you won't need much or be any trouble" to the travel representative. Word choice and labels are important aspects of Channel One. What something or someone is labeled has significant impact on how a message is received. The word choice in the following messages from parent to child are what distinguishes them and what determines the child's potential response.

"You're such a slob. Clean up your room."

"Please get your room cleaned up by dinner time."

Word choice in the second message does a clearer job of labeling the problem as residing in the messy room rather than in the child.

The subtleties of word choice sometimes escape us because words that are red flags for others may not be so for us. Offensive words may only be offensive to the receiver. The civil rights and women's consciousness-raising movements of the 1960s and 1970s sensitized us to the effect words like "girl" and "boy" have on those that are so labeled. The choice of "Miss," "Mrs.," or "Ms," for example, can carry significant meaning.

Upset people usually select words that reflect their feelings. Large numbers and imperatives pepper their speech. Phrases like "this is the hundredth time," "you never," "you always," "you have to," "you must" indicate that someone is upset.

Jargon

Occupational groups, social groups and family groups all have languages that only group members really understand. This language, jargon, provides useful shorthand for the members. The problem, however, usually lies in the fact that non-group members don't speak the same language. A critical aspect of word choice is remembering not to use *your* group's jargon with non-group members. Violation of this rule can provoke upset in others and certainly is not useful in defusing anger or grief in people who are already upset. For example, clients should be directed to "please complete this application form for assistance with your problem" as opposed to "we'll need to have your RBS 222 on file before we can help you." Similarly, the new babysitter you hire may need to be told specific words your children use related to food, playthings, bathroom habits, etc. Otherwise "need t–t" may be valueless gibberish to the sitter who rushes Johnny to the bathroom when he was requesting tinkertoys or tasty-treats. You can prevent some potential upset in people by serving as a translator of your jargon into language that can be more easily understood.

Written Communication

A final word about the language channel. Channel One is the only channel available to us for written communication. When we are writing, we have no way to soften a blow or clarify a point with our tone or expression. This means that word choice is particularly critical in letters, memos, notes, reports etc. Certainly when writing important messages, it can be a good idea to have someone who is unfamiliar with the message read or edit it for meaning and interpretation. When you are rereading your own written material, be sure to put yourself in the potential reader's shoes. Look for alternatives other than a letter or memo whenever possible.

In summary, Channel One is the foundation of communication. Word choice, labels and jargon can assist or impede communication. This channel is particularly sensitive in written communication.

Channel Two: Manner

The second channel of communication is the manner channel. Just as Channel One is the "what" of communication, Channel Two is the "how." Tone of voice, clarity, intonation and pace determine the way messages are transmitted.The words we choose are important, but in oral communication, how we vocalize the words may be even more important. If Channels One and Two do not send the same message, receivers always believe Channel Two over Channel One. The travel person's manner (described in the opening paragraph of this chapter) took precedence over her initial helpful words. Good communicators, when sending messages,make certain that Channels One and Two are consistent.

Channel Two and Feelings

Channel Two tells us a lot about the feeling state of others. People who are upset often send messages about their upset by "how" they communicate. Any exaggeration of tone, clarity, intonation or pace is what we observe. People who speak too fast or too slow; people who enunciate too clearly or very little; people who speak too softly or very loudly are sending cues that something is amiss. Changes on the manner channel are also significant indicators about feelings. As people's feelings change, their pace, tone, clarity and inflection change.

Telephone Contact

Telephone contact uses Channels One and Two. The telephone blocks visual clues. Therefore, because most of us use the telephone regularly, we need to be aware of the impact of Channel Two on our communication. We need to substitute verbal behaviors for behaviors that can't be seen over the phone.

> An administrative aide was well regarded and considered personable and helpful by most of the people with whom she had contact. However, there were occasional complaints from individuals who had never met her prior to a phone conversation. In analyzing the problem, it became clear that her voice had a flat quality

which was interpreted as anger or disinterest. In face-to-face contact her warmth transcended her voice quality because of her smiles, facial expression and gestures. Voice training using audio tapes as feedback proved helpful.

In summary, Channel Two has a great impact on oral communication. On the telephone, visual cues are missing. Therefore Channels One and Two are our primary transmitters. Upset people often use Channel Two to express the magnitude of their feelings. As a receiver it is important to scan Channel Two for indications of how others are feeling. As a sender, it is important to match Channels One and Two to make sure you are heard correctly.

Channel Three: Body Language

The third channel of communication is body language. Facial expression, eye contact, gestures and posture make up Channel Three. If Channel One is what we say and Channel Two is how we say it vocally, then Channel Three is how we say it visually. Smiles, tears or clenched fists tell us a lot about people. In face-to-face contact we utilize the first three channels to get a reading of the other person's emotional state. Like Channel Two, Channel Three is often a better indicator of how someone is feeling than is Channel One. Channels Two and Three together are the clearest yardsticks of emotion. Sending the same message on all three channels is what we strive for as good communicators. Good listeners use their ears and eyes to discern the message on Channels Two and Three.

Changes in Body Language

Reading another person's body language, while important, can also be overdone. Sometimes people cross their arms simply because they don't know what else to do with them. It might be a mistake to interpret these gestures as meaning the person is "closed" to communicating with us or is going to be "a tough nut to crack." On the other hand, a noticeable change or shift in a person's body language provides a gauge of their feelings.

> Mary made an appointment with the university's financial aid office. She appeared friendly and relaxed with the counselor while discussing her financial situation. A question about her father's vocation, however, caused Mary to shift uncomfortably in her chair. She began clearing her throat and stuttering slightly. The financial aid counselor noticing this, learned through questions that Mary's father had recently had a stroke. Her father's disability necessitated that Mary solve her financial dilemma as quickly as possible. Reading Channel Two and Channel Three helped the counselor gain difficult to talk about personal information which was pertinent for determining her need.

All of us can gather and utilize valuable information about others' feelings through observation. If we scan Channel Three, most of us find we can predict the moods of loved ones and friends — sometimes by their footsteps and posture alone. Interestingly, one of the things we are aware of as we write this book is the difficulty of describing Channels Two and Three when the written word, Channel One, is the only tool at our disposal. When presenting this information in seminar form, we can demonstrate Channels Two and Three by using them. To have only one channel on which to communicate is limiting.

In summary, Channel Three, body language, helps us to read messages from others through visual cues. People tell us a lot about what they are thinking and feeling through facial expressions, gestures and postures. In addition to taking an overall reading of ourselves and others in interactions, it is essential to observe changes in body language and to consider them a barometer of changes in feeling.

Channel Four: Territory

The fourth channel of communication is one of territory. Channel Four is the mode of communication related to the use of physical space and the management of personal physical and psychological territory.

Personal Space: Physical

All people have functionally distinct areas of physical space surrounding them. The core area around each of us (anything less than about 18 inches) is our intimate zone. There are only two ways a person should ever enter another person's intimate zone. The first is by invitation. Invitation means that Channels One, Two and Three say "come on in." The only other reason for being in another person's intimate zone is by function. Two or more people working together on something that requires closeness may require a working distance less than 18 inches. When a person inappropriately enters someone's intimate zone, the focus and goal of the invaded person becomes one of removing the intruder from the intimate zone. No real communication is possible under these circumstances.

From 18 inches to 36 inches is the territory within which "business" is conducted. It is about the distance of a handshake. Beyond 36 inches is stranger territory. It is very difficult to have significant communication in stranger territory. People have been known to become upset when personal or business communication has been attempted across too wide an area. The physician's receptionist who announces test results across the waiting room filled with patients or the bank teller who announces an overdrawn account to a customer several yards away is violating good communication practices. So, too, is the parent who continually reprimands publicly or the spouse who belittles the partner at social gatherings.

Personal Space: Psychological

Each of us has psychological zones similar to our physical zones. Our core psychological space is made up of things that significantly define who we are. People who put much of their energy into a career or people who are very invested parents have these roles embedded in their core psychological area. The next ring in our personal psychological space includes those roles and definitions about ourselves that we consider a part of us but are not crucial. For example, some men and women might designate parenthood in the core psychological territory while placing community activities in the secondary area. Beyond our symbolic 36 inch psychological territory are those things that are not a part of our identity at all — the "not-me" qualities. Just as a person may feel attacked if his or her core psychological territory is invaded, so he or she might feel attacked if the "not-me" qualities are attributed to him or her.

> A friend of ours is an artist who has also become extremely successful through the recognition of her work and also because of her excellent skills at marketing. Because she thinks of herself as an artist and not as a businesswoman, she dismisses the skillful marketer part as just luck. She chooses to have the role of businesswoman in the "not-me" psychological space. She would take offense at being referred to as a good businesswoman. She is pleased when called a good artist.

Territory and Upset Persons

Psychological and physical territory are critical when we are dealing with upset people. In making positive contact, we need to recognize the other person's territory and be careful to not invade it. If we have already overstepped our bounds, we have to get out of the territory as quickly and carefully as possible. Upset is frequently the response to territorial invasion.

Non-personal Physical Territory

The arrangement and utilization of the physical space around us has implications for communication. We can become irritated if there are insufficient cues telling us where to go in order to accomplish our purpose efficiently. Furniture can be either a communication barrier or a useful and comfortable part of our space. The appropriate use of physical territory involves arranging it to maximize function and to minimize emotional backlash. In order to accomplish this satisfactorily, it is necessary to be clear on goals. How close do you want others, physically and psychologically? What will maximize the efficient flow of work? What do you want your space to say to others? These are questions that need answering.

> A large national company was set up physically so that many customers had to walk by the break room on their way to get service. Service representatives wondered why customers were so angry if they had to wait even a few minutes. An objective analysis of their territory suggested that customers believed that the wait was the result of service representatives sitting around and drinking coffee. After the break room was moved out of the traffic pattern, customers showed less irritation at short waits.

Territorial Rules

Here are some territorial rules to keep in mind:

1) Space is divided more or less equally among the number of individuals who share it. (Observe people on elevators.)

2) The less physical space available to us, the more we utilize psychological barriers to provide privacy. (Think about differences in people's behavior with strangers on the street in crowded urban areas and on the street of a small rural community.)

3) Physical territory often serves a symbolic purpose. (Observe the offices of executives, as opposed to the work areas of entry-level employees.)

4) A person can compensate for some territorial problems by how they position themselves. (Observe how people stay behind barriers when they want distance and come out from behind them when they don't.)

5) For maximum communication, advance to the edge of your territory and invite other people to come to the edge of theirs. Escort people into your space in order to be able to escort them out. (Observe your feelings when the person with whom you have an appointment greets you and takes you into the office versus being told, "Go to the third office on the left."

In summary, Channel Four, territory, is an important communication channel, especially as it relates to upset people. Personal territory and physical territory can be managed so as to enhance personal and business relationships.

Channel Five: Symbolic Communication

The fifth channel of communication is the channel that symbolically carries messages we want to send. Symbolic communication provides a shorthand way for each of us to send a lot of information about ourselves. A wedding band is easy to wear and not nearly as awkward as announcing our marital status in every new situation.

Dress

The style of clothes we wear is one component of symbolic communication. At an informal level, we say a lot about ourselves and our roles through the way we dress. Male executives symbolically communicate their role by coats and ties. We don't expect to find our plumber similarly dressed. Working outfits and uniforms can be functionally symbolic such as painter pants or a stethoscope around the neck. They also can be symbolic only. The painter pants and scrub uniforms worn by adolescents in the early 1980's made only symbolic statements and served no functional purpose.

People tell us a lot about themselves through their personal choice in clothing. A man in a business suit, a man in jeans and a man in fitted Italian casual wear are each sending a different symbolic message.

Utilizing Symbolic Messages

Symbolic messages are all around us. Cars, jewelry, hair-styles, photographs, credit cards and home decor say a lot about their owners. The task when sending messages is to be sure our symbolic choices send the appropriate and intended message. If we want to be taken seriously as a business person, we wear appropriate business clothes. If we are talking with people from a blue-collar background, we don't use personal examples about housekeepers or children's college experiences. If we are talking to an elderly hard-of-hearing person, we symbolically communicate respect by asking him to let us know if he's having trouble hearing. When we give customers and clients our business card, we are symbolically stating that we are accessible. Wiping our feet before entering someone's home can be a symbolic (as well as a practical) gesture.

We also must scan Channel Five carefully to receive the symbolic messages of other people. If we call on a friend whose home is filled with pictures of family or filled with bowling trophies and we don't comment on these items, we are missing the message and perhaps "the boat." Channel Five is invaluable in making positive contact and in dealing with upset people. When we observe that someone has spent time on personal grooming, we can feel more secure if we choose to comment sincerely on their appearance.

A young boy was brought before a juvenile judge for truancy and other delinquent behaviors. His parents, who were seated in the courtroom, were required to cooperate in the treatment process. The judge wishing to make a positive impact on the boy's life, said: "If you don't get a good education, you'll end up nothing more than a common laborer." You could see the father visibly wince as he sat in the courtroom in his denim overalls and workingman's boots. By not being sensitive to information sent on Channel Five, the judge was disregarding important symbolic information and perhaps costing parental cooperation.

In summary, Channel Five, the symbolic communication channel, allows each of us to say a lot about ourselves in shorthand. Channel Five tells us what is important to people.

Channel Six: Feelings

The sixth channel of communication is the feeling channel. Feelings get communicated through Channels One, Two and Three. In dealing with upset people, it is critical to understand and respond to the feelings of others. Much will be said about this in subsequent chapters, when we describe methods for dealing with upset people, angry people and people experiencing a loss.

Static

Unattended feelings represent static on the channels. When there is a lot of static on any receiver (TV, radio, C.B., or two-way) it is impossible for messages to get through. This is certainly the case in interpersonal communication. "Noise" from feelings blocks the messages. When our own feelings are running high, we must manage our own static. (Managing our own upset is covered in Chapter Four). The feelings of others provide static, too. It is difficult to hear the message under the feelings. The upset person cannot hear any rational input from us until the static (the feelings) is quieted. Profanity, crying, ugly gestures, yelling and over-enunciating all obscure the sender's message and block our ability to deal with the issues. Success in dealing with people who are upset is intimately tied to the ability to attend to people's feelings before dealing with specific issues or problems.

In summary, Channel Six is the feeling component in people's communication and is carried on Channels One, Two and Three. Feelings are received as static obscuring the real messages. Meaningful communication cannot take place until feelings are addressed.

Channel Seven: Behavior

The seventh and final channel of communication is our behavior — our intentional (and sometimes not so intentional) actions. While what we say and how we say it *is* important, what we do becomes the bottom line determinant of successful relationships.

It is important to do what we say we will do. For example, if we tell someone we care about them and like being with them, those words are meaningless unless we arrange to spend time together. Similarly, if we say our faith is important to us while neither involving ourselves in religious activities nor leading our lives based on the tenets of our faith, we are not behaving consistently with what we say is significant to us.

We never make promises we can't keep nor threats we don't have the power or inclination to execute. Rather than threaten, we inform. We inform our children of the potential consequences of rule breaking. We inform others about what they can and cannot expect us to do. If we can't keep a promise, we inform the person to whom we made the promise that we are no longer able to carry it out. For the most successful interactions, use follow-through and follow-up. In summary, Channel Seven says that what we do is the bottom line of the communication process.

The Seven Channels

The seven channels of communication described above are the basic building blocks of communication. All interactions include these seven channels in both sending and receiving. Good communicators successfully send the same message on all seven channels while scanning the channels of other people to be sure they are receiving the intended message.

Channels Three (body language), Five (symbolic communication), and Six (feelings) come into focus first. We look to see who the approaching people are, the ways in which they present themselves and what feelings they engender in us. At an almost subconscious level we determine territorial issues. Eventually we decode their message by scanning Channels One (language), Two (manner), and Three (body language).

Communication is a complex process. Like driving a car, we have been at it so long that we put the components together without much thought. As you focus on handling upset people, we ask you purposefully to be more aware of your's and other people's channels of communication.

■

CHAPTER THREE
TRANSACTIONAL ANALYSIS

THREE

In the middle of a seemingly pleasant family dinner, Jack described a remodeling project he had in mind for turning the basement into a small usable study. Jack's grown son began making suggestions about how Jack should carry out the project. First he told Jack he should consider putting the study where the garage was rather than in the basement in order to have a room with windows. Then Jack's son and his wife both said that they didn't think walnut paneling would be attractive. Within five minutes Jack's temper erupted and after shouting that he would fix his house "any darn way I want," he left the table and slammed out of the house to take a walk and cool down. When he returned, his son, daughter-in-law and wife all told him he was "acting like a baby." Jack ended up quietly angry and sullen the rest of the evening. No one left the dinner feeling good.

Conflict situations often seem to be wild, unpredictable happenings. When we are a part of the upset, we can feel totally helpless and out of control. Yet there *is* an understandable order in what appears to be chaos. We don't have to be as helpless as we feel. Understanding what is happening to the other person as well as what is happening to ourselves can help us to be more in charge of ourselves and to help others regain control of themselves. What we need in order to understand this process is a framework or a model within which upset can be better understood. This chapter presents just such a model — one that will help us to understand what works best for dealing with upset people.

Transactional Analysis

Transactional analysis (T.A.) is a model for understanding how people communicate. Eric Berne, the originator of T.A., defined a transaction as a unit of social interaction; a unit of communication. T.A. helps us to think about what happens in our communication with other people. It also helps us to figure out how to change our communication so that we can prevent and manage upset in other people. In other words, once we understand these transactions, we can also improve them.

Three different parts make up each of us. T.A. calls these parts Ego States. Which ego state we are in determines how we communicate. Think, for a moment, about a person in your life you know very well. You can usually visualize this person in a number of different ways. He or she might be laughing at something funny, looking depressed or feeling angry. You might picture this person talking to and petting a dog. Perhaps the person is scolding a child for talking back. Finally, you might imagine this person at a business meeting conducting himself or herself with propriety while making a staff presentation and fielding questions. It might be difficult to remember that this reasonable, effective businessperson was having a temper tantrum over a scraped fender just the night before. Each of us has many dimensions. According to T.A., the various aspects of our personalities can be classified into three states: the child state, the parent state and the adult state.

Because we all have these different ego states, every person has the potential to communicate in a variety of ways. We can be playful, serious, rational, loving, concerned, angry and critical. Communication out of certain ego states is more effective when dealing with people who are upset. More about this shortly, First, let's talk about each of the three states.

The Child Ego State

The child part of us focuses on getting our needs met. The child in each of us is small, clumsy, dependent and without words. Since this little person within us lacks words, reactions are all in the form of feelings. It is the body of feelings related to being dependent and trying to get our needs met that we carry through life with us in the form of our child ego state. We are moved into our child state anytime our feelings are activated. Our child has the capacity to be angry, rebellious, frightened, happy, loving, sad and so forth. If these feelings are addressed and our needs are met, our child state can then let go of them. The goals of the child part of us are to be liked, to be admired, to have fun and to have needs met. All of our feelings, wishes, wants and needs can be found in our child ego state. You can already see that when you are dealing with upset people, you are dealing with people who are talking to you out of their child ego state.

The Manipulative Child

In addition to our natural child state, we each also have within us what, in T.A., is called a manipulative child. Sometimes in the process of having our needs met as children, we learned behaviors that we then try to utilize to get our needs met later in life.

> As a small child, Philip's mother would frequently break down and let Philip have his way after he carried on and screamed so long that she felt she could stand no more. As an adult, Philip escalates his abrasive anger higher and higher when he is crossed. In most cases, Philip can hold out longer than the other person and he ends up getting his way.

The part of our child ego state that uses manipulation to get needs met is called the "manipulative child." We must be careful not to reward upset people who are escalating unacceptable behaviors and operating out of their manipulative child state. If we are going to meet their requests, we need to do so before they feel the need to engage in trantrum-like behavior. If we do not plan to meet their requests, we must not allow ourselves to be intimidated into changing our minds.

It is wise to initially approach an upset individual as if his or her upset is genuine — real feelings of distress coming from the natural child. The formulas and techniques described in later chapters outline the kinds of responses that work to calm upset people. When we respond to a person's upset with appropriate understanding and helpfulness and they continue to stay upset or even to increase their upset behavior, in all likelihood, we are seeing the manipulative child part of the person in action.

Upset people are almost always in their child ego state. This ego state (their feelings) must be addressed before any problems can be handled. We'll have more to say about this in Chapter Seven.

The Parent Ego State

The parent state is so named because within each of us lies the capacity to love and to make rules about behavior — two capacities that good parenting demands. As parents, we love and care for our children. We also help them to learn right from wrong and to learn the rules and limits involved in being a part of a social system. Our own parent state is passed down to us from our parents and other significant people in our lives who have loved us and taught us. We take what we have learned and store it inside of us. These learnings become our parent ego state. They include how we love others and all the prohibitions, admonitions and rules both stated and set by example. We store these learnings without question. The goal of the parent ego state is to be superior, caring and helpful.

The Critical Parent

The parent ego state has two parts: the critical parent and the caring parent. The two parent states each has a different effect upon people who are upset. When a child falls and skins his or her knee, the parent may say to the child, "You shouldn't have been running so fast. If you'd been more careful, you wouldn't have hurt yourself."

Such a statement is typical of the critical parent.

All of the internal rules that govern us come from the critical parent. Most of the imperatives — you should, you must, you ought to, why can't you, don't you see — are pronounced by the critical parent embedded within each of us. Sometimes we don't even know why we carry these rules around and why we insist they should be applied in our present lives.

> I (Pennie) remember my mother teaching me how to make chicken soup — a skill no nurturing mother (we'll discuss nurturing in the next section) worth her salt is without. One of the family's unbreakable rules of chicken soup-making was that the soup had to be skimmed just after it came to a boil. For years, I followed this maternal "must." One day I raised the inevitable question. "Mom," I said, "why is it we always skim the soup after it comes to a boil?" Her answer was the classic demonstration of how parental messages are transferred from one generation to another — this parental message being one she learned by example rather than by verbal rule. She said, "When I was a child my grandmother, who was very poor, always skimmed the soup. Since she never threw away anything edible, I just assumed the skimmed part of the soup must be inedible." So much for that "should." I either had to learn a more significant reason to skim chicken soup or not shake my finger at myself in a critical parent way if I chose to avoid this step.

The Caring Parent

Now that we've observed what our critical parent part

says when a child skins his or her knee, let's look at the response of the caring parent. The caring parent says to that same child with tenderness and kindness, "Oh, you skinned your knee. I'll bet it hurts. Let's wash it off carefully and put a bandage on it."

Each of us carries both a critical parent and a caring parent within us. The problem in dealing with upset people is that sometimes our natural inclination is to respond out of the critical parent when in fact we would do much better to respond out of the caring parent. The friend who is disappointed by your inability to share a last minute dinner invitation will react better to a simple "I'm sorry we'll miss having dinner together" than to "If you had called me earlier in the week, then I'd have had time to get a sitter." The feelings of the child state get handled most satisfactorily when we respond as a caring parent. The formula for handling upset people in Chapter Seven will say more about this.

The Adult Ego State

The third ego state is the adult ego state. The adult is the rational part of us. It gathers and processes data. It begins developing when we are very young. Our life experiences give us new information that challenge both the taught concepts of the parent and the feelings of the child. The adult part of us figures things out by looking at facts. It is unemotional. The goal of the adult is to be competent.

A common mistake in dealing with an upset person is to behave from the adult ego state too soon. Since upset people are in their child ego state, they need a caring parent. Once our caring parent has dealt with the child's (the upset person's) feelings then we can successfully move into the adult ego state and turn our attention to solving the problem presented.

Each of us is made up of all three parts. All of the ego states are equally important. None is superior. However, it is helpful to use our caring parent ego state to attend to the feelings of upset people and our adult ego state to assess situations and to make decisions and to solve problems.

Transactional Analysis and Upset People

In the story that opened this chapter, Jack's family may have thought they were behaving as logical, rational adults, but they were talking as critical parents. And, as is almost always the case when we are lectured by critical parents, Jack responded as an upset, angry child. If Jack was hoping for either approval (caring parent) or adult suggestions, he was disappointed. He was left feeling inadequate and defensive. Anyone at this dinner could have positively affected the outcome if they had understood what was happening and managed their behavior accordingly. "You've clearly put a lot of learning into this project." "It's great to see you so enthusiastic about the new room." "Sounds like you are looking forward to getting started." T.A. provides a useful model for understanding ourselves and other people. It can help us to defuse a potentially difficult situation by:

Step 1: responding from the caring parent state to address the feelings of the upset person

Step 2: moving to the adult state to solve the problem that created the upset. If there is no problem to be solved only step one is necessary

Success in dealing with upset people involves avoiding these mistakes:

Mistake #1: Using your critical parent rather than your caring parent

Mistake #2: Skipping over the caring parent phase and moving too quickly to your adult

Mistake #3: Responding from your child

It is not easy to stay in charge of ourselves, set an appropriate tone for interactions and remain open and nondefensive. Yet, this is the key to dealing with upset people.

■

CHAPTER FOUR
DEALING WITH OUR OWN UPSET

FOUR

Marge, a nurse in a long term care facility, confided that the person whose upset she has the hardest time dealing with is her own. She described two incidents that really bothered her. The first incident took place on a day when she was exhausted — the end of an especially busy and tiring shift. The daughter of a patient attacked Marge, berating and belittling her about the poor care she felt her mother was receiving. The criticism hurt and angered Marge — especially when she felt she had just given the patients her "all" for eight hours. The second incident took place a few weeks after Marge's own mother had moved into a long term care facility. When a patient began to complain to Marge about how her children had abandoned her, Marge said she felt so guilty and defensive she could not continue to listen.

Both incidents that Marge reported represent some of difficult situations most of us face in the course of our work or our personal lives. Because we too are human, our own physical and emotional states play a role in how we handle the upset of other people. The natural tendency to get upset ourselves in the face of another person's upset is more likely to occur when our own needs need tending, when the upset person attacks us or when the fires of our own personal problems are fueled by what the upset person is saying.

Before we can share our ideas on how to deal with upset people, the issue of how to deal with our own upset needs to be examined. We have to be able to handle ourselves if we are going to use the six principles for dealing with upset people. These principles, in summary involve:

- handling the situation in such a way that our self-esteem and the other person's self esteem are not damaged and are perhaps even enhanced.

- recognizing that we are very important to the outcome of the situation.

- staying in charge of ourselves by managing our own behavior.

- fighting the natural tendency to get upset with upset people.

- insuring that the original cause of the upset doesn't turn into secondary upset — upset related to how we treated the other person's upset.

- working at the softest level possible to defuse the situation.

This chapter will focus on how to deal with our own feelings of upset: how to prevent them; how to manage them when they exist; and for the occasions when we are less than perfect, what to do after an incident where our own upset has leaked out.

The Before: Preventing and Minimizing One's Own Upset

Our reactions to upset people are affected by a number of things, including our expectations, our value systems, our past experiences, our perceptions, the meaning we attach to things and the way in which we talk to ourselves. We become upset when we expect people always to behave well; never to feel or show negative emotions such as upset, anger, withdrawal, sadness or grief. Our values can play in a part in our feelings too. For example, if we value an "always feel and look happy stance," then we get upset by people who experience and or demonstrate feelings that are upsetting in nature. If we have been unsuccessful in defusing upset people in the past, if we have felt overwhelmed or intimidated by upset people in the past or if we have had bad situations become worse in the past, then we are more likely to talk to ourselves in negative ways — continuing to upset ourselves rather than preparing ourselves to approach the upsetting situation constructively.

Activity for Preventing and Minimizing One's Own Upset

Think about those things that trigger your own upset and anger. These triggers for upset are often called "hot buttons." Our hot buttons are those things that tend to set off our emotions. Mary A, the nurse in the chapter's opening story could put at least three items on her personal hot button list: 1) When I'm tired I tend to get more easily upset: 2) when I feel I've been helpful, it upsets me when someone criticizes me by saying I have not been helpful; and 3) when I'm feeling guilty and unsure about some action I've taken, I get easily upset if someone suggests that my action might not have been appropriate.

Start a list of your hot buttons. If you do not know your own hot buttons, ask those closest to you, "what are the things you think tend to trigger my anger, my hurt, my upset?" Also notice what people say to you when you think they are wanting to upset you. If your manager calls you "too perfectionistic" or "lazy" or "always late finishing your projects" and you immediately feel angry and defensive, these phrases may be your hot buttons. Likewise, if, in the midst of a domestic quarrel, the phrase "you're just like you father" has you see red, such a phrase belongs on your hot button list.

Once you have identified some of your hot buttons, then list expectations, values and past experiences you believe contribute to your own upsetting feelings. If you can identify a link between the current feeling and a hot button, an expectation, a value or a past experience, just the recognition that your feeling is triggered by something other than the current situation will help reduce your upset. Moreover, once you have identified some of the things that typically upset you, you can plan new ways of reacting to particular situations.

The During: What To Do In The Midst Of Upset

Assuming that you are already experiencing upset, what can you do to help yourself. The first step is to acknowledge and own your feelings. "Am I angry?" "Am I depressed?" "Am I hurt?" "Defensive?" "Scared?" Tune in to yourself. Try to identify the feeling. If you know specifically **what** you are feeling and **what** might be creating that feeling then the most successful approach for managing our own upset is to develop an inner dialogue which helps to calm us rather than having us react to the upset of other people. One way to develop such an appropriate inner dialogue is to use rational thinking. Rational thinking comes from our adult ego state. Upset, as you may recall, comes from our child ego state. One particular method for changing the inner dialogue from a child dialogue to an adult dialogue comes from a psychological theory called rational-emotive therapy (RET) formulated by Albert Ellis. According to Ellis, irrational thinking is responsible for a great deal of human discomfort. Our anxieties could be reduced significantly if we talked to ourselves rationally.

Four Irrational Beliefs

Ellis describes four kinds of human irrational beliefs that can lead to getting upset. Irrational beliefs can come from an erroneous belief that certain things "must happen" or else we will be upset. "I must do well." "I must be approved of." "I must get what I want." If these "musts" do not happen, then I will be upset. Irrational thinking can also spring from "awfulizing," "can't stand its," and "damning of yourself and others." The inner dialogues of these irrationalities go something like this:

> "It's awful when someone is upset. If my client is upset with me, she'll probably never do business with me again."

> "If my supervisor corrects me in front of the other guys, I won't be able to stand the humiliation. I just don't know what I'll do. I won't be able to stand it."

> "I hate myself for not knowing exactly what to say to John about his divorce." How can I be so dumb? I never do anything right."

You can see how these irrational beliefs keep us upset rather than helping us to be less upset.

The ABC'S

Ellis teaches what he calls the ABC's of behavior. An **A**ctivating Event (A) seems to cause an emotional reaction or Consequence (C) in people. However, A does not really cause C. On closer inspection, it becomes clear that C was more likely caused by the **Belief System (B)** or how people talk to themselves.

Let's look at an example of how this might work. The spouse of a friend from work suddenly dies. This is the activating experience. You want to make a condolence call on your friend. Your inner dialogue might be:

> This is a painful time for Mary. I'd like to go see her to express my sadness for her, my caring and to let her know I'll be around if she needs something. If I put myself in her shoes, I'd appreciate the visit and expressions of sympathy. I don't need to *do* anything. I just need to go and be there.

With an inner dialogue or belief system like the one above, you are likely to go to see Mary (the appropriate consequence) with little anxiety because you haven't placed enormous expectations on yourself. All you have to do is pay a visit and be there for her. This visit most likely meets Mary's needs and your needs. How might the same scenario play out if you employ irrational beliefs or faulty self-talk at step B? In that case your inner dialogue might be:

> I want to go to see Mary, but I'm not sure she wants me to do that. What will I say to her? It's always so hard to think of the right things to say to someone who is grieving. What if she cries? What if I cry? What if she thinks I have ulterior motives? Maybe she'll think I didn't know her husband well enough to pay a condolence visit. Maybe there will be so many people there she won't notice that I came and I'll feel left out.

With this kind of inner dialogue you are placing tremendous expectations on yourself and Mary. The result or consequence of such self-talk is likely to be one that will not mutually meet your needs or Mary's needs. You are likely to decide not to pay the call or, if you do make the visit, you may be self-conscious and lack spontaneity. Worse yet, you may place inappropriate expectations on a grieving friend and become disappointed in how she responds to your visit. Your expectations are unlikely to be met. Mary may lose the comfort of a caring friend. Any of these consequences would be inappropriate.

We hope it is clear from the above example that self-talk rather than the activating event is responsible for the behavioral outcome. Our inner dialogue results in us being either upset or not upset. We must move into our adult state if we are to manage our own upset. Ellis suggests that if faulty inner dialogues and irrational beliefs keep us upset, then we must Dispute (D) those irrational ideas in our heads in order to produce a new and more desirable consequence or Effect (E). Imagine a sarcastic, upset customer approaching a service representative at a local utility company.

> "I don't know why I had to wait ten minutes to get. through to you. You'd think with the outrageous rates consumers pay for electricity, this company could hire enough employees."

How does the service representative talk to herself? The child in her, using an irrational belief, might feel picked on unfairly or somehow feel responsible for the customer's upset. Placating or defensive behavior might result. A more rational inner dialogue, with a better result or effect, would be:

> "This man is upset about his high electric bill. He is not angry with me. I do not have to solve all his financial problems. Nor do I have to defend myself or my company. I do have to acknowledge, understand and respond to his feelings. I will do my best to help him to solve his problem."

Activity for Improving Rational Thinking

A. Describe an event that in the past has activated your upset.

B. Write down what you have said to yourself about this event in the past.

C. What do you usually do based on the way in which you have spoken to yourself?

D. Write out something different from B above that you could say to yourself to dispute your irrational belief.

E. How do you think you will feel and how do you imagine you'll behave if you are successful in replacing D for B — disputing your irrational belief with a more rational one.

Rational Self-Talk and Upset People

Dealing with upset people requires that we *not* operate out of the child or critical parent ego state. Therefore, some kind of internal mechanism is needed to help control natural, instinctive, but unproductive behaviors. Behavior is motivated by what people say to themselves. This suggests that anger and hurt, as well as other feelings, are a choice. If upset feelings are a choice, we can choose to respond to upset people in a variety of other ways. We have the choice of getting angry, becoming hostile or yelling. We also can choose alternative behaviors by talking to ourselves in such a way as to control the level of our upset. When we talk to ourselves rationally, we are more successful in our dealings with upset people.

Paths of Expression

There are many ways to handle and express upset while in the midst of experiencing it. One tool used by successful communicators is the "time out."

A high level manager who worked his way up through the ranks of a moderate sized company describes using the "time out" to handle upset in the following way. "If I feel a strong emotional reaction taking over my ability to think clearly, I always ask the other person for some time to think. My rule of thumb for this time out is at least 15 minutes and never more than a day. Fifteen minutes gives me time to regain my composure. I find if I wait longer than 24 hours, I tend to not get around to following up. When I use a time out, I usually say 'give me 15 minutes, an hour or until tomorrow and I'll get back to you.' And then I do get back to them."

While each of us uses the channels of communication to express feelings, we vary in how we use them. Some of us are quite vocal, relying heavily on the language channel. Some of us sigh, raise our voices, slow or hasten our speech, use sarcasm or stay silent, relying on the manner channel. Use of the territory channel is the province of those who walk out, slam doors or get too close for comfort. The body language channel is employed by the eye-rollers and fist shakers. Be aware of your preferred modes of expression. You might experiment to find more appropriate and effective ways to express your upset.

The After: What To Do After The Upset

Just as the morning after "hangover" and the morning after "guilt" is familiar to the person who drank too much the night before, so too we often suffer the most after an upsetting incident is over. We may feel guilty; we may feel embarrassed; we may feel like we overreacted; we may feel angry at ourselves. It is not unusual for people to continuously replay the incident — often non-productively.

A Cure For The Hangover

The best cure for the bad feelings that come after one has been upset is to let go of the incident and to let go of the guilt that often accompanies having gotten upset. Guilt is an important feeling when it serves the purpose of stopping us in advance from engaging in behaviors we know we should not undertake. Recognizing potential guilty feelings in advance acts as a deterrent to negative behaviors. For example, many of us don't yell some of the nasty things we momentarily feel at our loved ones because experience has taught us that everyone, including us, suffers if we do. This kind of guilt, we'd label constructive guilt. Destructive guilt, in contrast, does not change our behavior. In fact, by beating ourselves after the fact, we may actually feel we are "putting in the time" for "doing the crime." Such "after the fact" guilt may even have us feel we can go ahead and behave poorly again because we have already paid for our last bout of misbehavior.

If you have lost your cool and gotten upset in a way that feels truly anti-productive or upset in a way that feels embarrassing, stop replaying the incident in your mind. Letting go of the incident can be accomplished by using the rational talk described earlier in the chapter or by the following two suggestions for finding safe dump sites and making the appropriate recycling effort.

Safe Dump Sites

Safe dump sites are those places where you can unload your upset feelings without doing further damage.

Sometimes, other people provide safe dump sites. When we are upset with our boss at work, we may be able to complain angrily to the friend or spouse who is a good listener. Frustration with our clumsy four year old may be vented with a close friend or the parent of another four year old who understands our frustration with spilled milk and messy play areas.

Most of us learn who in our lives are safe for dumping and who are not. Avoid those people who are likely to use their critical parent rather than their caring parent. Also, it usually is not safe to dump on someone who is directly effected by our upset. These people include those who are the objects of the upset and those who may respond defensively because of over identification with the problem. It is unlikely to be safe to complain about the customer who is places hard-to-fill last minute orders to a friend who asks for last minute favors.

There are as many safe dumping sites as the imagination permits. Punching bags and soft pillows can be pounded. Bowling pins can be aimed at as if they were the person with whom we're upset. Slamming a racquetball, riding a bike and running can siphon off upset feelings. Spectator sports allow us to yell safely. Praying, singing, listening to music provide many of us with a release. Talking to ourselves and writing letters we never send are also examples of safe dump sites for our upset feelings.

Recycling

Once our upset is behind us, the best thing we can do is

use the past to help us in the future. Can we now identify a "hot button" and use this knowledge to minimize future upset by planning a new behavior to use when that hot button is activated? Can we recognize the non-productive self-talk that only fanned the flames of our upset and plan to replace it with more rational self-talk? Can we figure out how to avoid certain upsetting situations in the future? For example, should we plan short weekend visits to our in-laws rather than week long visits? Can we remember the guilt from a past incident and therefore decide to change our future behavior — using the guilt as a constructive deterrent? "Recycling" is related to "curing the hangover." It is productive to use a past upsetting incident to prevent a future one.

■

CHAPTER FIVE
PREVENTING UPSET

FIVE

Peter and Marilyn Gold were a gracious host and hostess. They had a knack for putting together interesting groups of people and for giving successful parties. An evening at the Gold's always began with Pete and Marilyn greeting their guests at the door, introducing them to other guests previously unknown to them and showing them to the food and drinks. Pete and Marilyn knew that the success of the evening often depended on how the evening began.

An ounce of prevention is worth a pound of cure. Similarly, when interactions get off on a good footing, it lessens the likelihood of having to deal with an upset person. Making positive contact is the obvious first step in any conversation. Before discussing the specific elements of positive contact, let's take a look at two components of the interpersonal process that affect our ability to connect positively with others and to interact successfully with them.

Liking People

Most people like to be liked. The need to be liked is based on the fact that people are dependent upon one another for survival. During infancy basic survival needs must be met by other people. Throughout our lives, each of us requires a variety of people to meet some of our physical, emotional, social and sexual needs. This interdependency makes it necessary for us to like people and for people to like us.

Virginia Satir, a well-known family therapist, describes each of us as having a pot of good feelings about ourself that we can hoard or share with others. The more full our pot, the more we have to share. If our pot is almost empty, we have very little to give away. People with empty pots don't feel good about themselves and don't feel good about other people. Having few good feelings about ourselves gets in the way of our ability to relate to people. We have more trouble liking other people and they have more trouble liking us. When we have good feelings to give to others, then they have more good feelings back to us. Therefore, one way to replenish our own pot is by filling other people's pots. Reaching out and making positive contact helps us to like others and therefore to like ourselves better. The couple in our opening illustration will no doubt have the opportunity to be future guests at other social gatherings. Being positive and outgoing hosts will indirectly impact their self-esteem.

A second element that affects our sociability originates in how we have been treated by significant people in our lives. If we have been treated badly, not only have we learned to not trust others, but we also have not learned how to make positive contact. Such a lack of trust and know-how interferes with our willingness and ability to approach others. A paradox exists here Holding back causes others to hold back. Following the principle of natural tendencies, aloofness begets aloofness. We are then reinforced in our belief that others are cold and distant and not to be trusted. Reaching out and making positive contact reinforces us positively because it produces positive behavior in others.

A third factor affecting our liking of people is a result of how we remember our past interactions with people. If we remember only negative interactions, we tend to view people negatively. The natural tendency is to remember the one or two negative interactions of the day rather than the eight or ten positive ones. This kind of selective recall has an impact on how we feel about people. Balanced memories of interactions with people lead to more positive feelings about them.

Finally, how we feel about others is affected by how we feel about what we do. It is important to like what we do — jobs, family life, recreation and hobbies. Time is the one resource that is distributed equally to everyone. The task is to be sure to do the best possible job of spending it.

Liking what we do relates to how well we do it. If our job does not satisfactorily address interests, aptitudes or personality, we may need to rethink career goals. If we recognize that much of our nonworking time is spent unsatisfactorily, it may be time to explore alternative lifestyle possibilities. It is not selfish to work toward liking what we do. How we feel about how we spend our life affects everyone our life touches. Obviously, no one is content with every aspect of life all the time. The goal is to make what we do count for us.

Letting People Know We Like Them

Liking people is only the first step in making positive contact. The second step is letting others know we like them. Each of us varies in our ability to reach out and become involved with people. The individual capacity to do this lies on a continuum. People on one end of the continuum find it very easy to show people they like them. People at the other end find it very difficult. People on the "easy" end of the continuum probably already know a lot about setting the tone and being in charge of interactions. They are also probably aware that their positive approach to other people is reciprocated. This, in turn, enhances self-confidence and self-esteem, making it even easier to continue to show liking for others. All in all, it is a very circular process.

Of course, the circular process may be a negative one for people who find it difficult to show others that they like them. This negative circularity reinforces the difficulty of reaching out to other people.

If you fall on the "difficult" end of the continuum, it probably means that you are either shy and fearful of rejection or that you have not cultivated your interpersonal skills to their fullest. In short, you're either scared or you don't know how. In either case, the only remedy is practice, practice and more practice.

Before reading on, please take time to assess yourself on the following shyness inventory. There is no score on this inventory. Rather, it is designed to have you stop and take stock of yourself in regard to shyness. You might also find it helpful to use this inventory as a feedback tool. Ask a loved one, a friend or a co-worker to share their perceptions of you by answering the questions on the inventory as they pertain to you. It can be helpful to learn how others see us.

Self-Assessment of Shyness

1) Is shyness ever a problem for you?

2) Have any of the following sometimes made you feel shy?

Fear of rejection	Fear of evaluation
Lack of confidence	Fear of intimacy
Lack of social skills	Personal inadequacies

3) Do other people see you as shy? Are you able to conceal your shyness?

4) Do other people see you as unfriendly or aloof?

5) Are there specific situations in which you feel shy? For example, in large groups; where you don't know anyone; where you are the center of attention; in social situations? List these.

6) Are you more shy around certain kinds of people? For example, around authorities; strangers; people of the opposite sex; relatives; people of different backgrounds? List these.

7) Do you experience physical reactions to shyness such as blushing, perspiring, heart-pounding? List these.

8) Do you think you are self-conscious?

9) Do you have difficulty making eye contact with people? Smiling at others? Introducing yourself?

10) Do you struggle talking to others? Do you speak too quietly; Do you have difficulty in thinking of anything to say? Are you silent? Do you stutter? Do you ramble? List these.

11) Are you aware of any personal consequences of your shyness? Costs? Benefits? List these.

The Tactful Acronym

If you like people and want them to know you like them, you already are well motivated for making positive contact. A useful frame of reference for making positive connections with people is an acronym that helps people remember seven key elements that comprise the process of reaching out to people. The acronym T-A-C-T-F-U-L is also a reminder that positive contact requires tact.

Territory

The "T" in TACTFUL stands for *territory*. Territory has been discussed in some detail in Chapter Two. The important positive contact premise about territory is to come to the edge of our territory and encourage other people to come to the edge of their's. Moving to the edge of our territory is accomplished physically by such things as taking community activities to the group who can best use the services, by coming out from behind a desk, by going to the door of an adolescent's room or by going to the home of a friend who is bereaved. Symbolically, we demonstrate being at the edge of our territory by doing as much as possible to be helpful without intruding: "May I hold your umbrella while you find what you need in your purse?" "Before we get any further, let me tell you what this volunteer job entails." An offer of Kleenex to a person who is crying or making eye contact with someone to indicate that we'll be with them shortly are examples of coming to the edge of our territory and inviting others to do likewise.

It is also important to communicate a respect for limits. We offer a chair without forcing a person to sit down. We indicate a willingness to listen without demanding a person talk. We knock at the door of an adolescent's room or a colleague's office, but we do not enter without an invitation. To reiterate, the guideline is to come to the edge of our territory, not to barge into someone else's territory.

Appropriate Facial Expression

While this is a well-known suggestion, it bears repeating. In our initial contact with people, it is important to greet them with an appropriate facial expression. In the absence of cues that would indicate otherwise, smiling is the most appropriate way to reach out nonverbally to others. A *smile* is a universal human connector. It is almost impossible to be unresponsive to a person who greets you with a smile. If you doubt this, try smiling to salespeople, people you pass in your work setting or shoppers at the grocery store. Practice smiling over the telephone. A smile can be heard over the telephone because our voices resonate higher when we are smiling. When we smile we are likely to bring out the positive in other people.

> When my (Don's) Grandmother Bertie first entered the nursing home where she lived the last twelve years of her life, she got the nickname "the you can give me something special lady." She'd approach various residents saying, "You know you can give me something special." "What can we give you when we have nothing to give?" they'd respond. Bertie would say, "You can give me a smile." In her quiet way, Bertie brought much joy to her Texas nursing home.

A smile is an appropriate facial expression in most, but not all, situations. Obviously we don't smile at angry, upset or grieving people. In such situations, our faces reflect concern.

Contact

The phrase, positive contact, reminds us of the universal need for *contact* between people. In order for a conversation to be successful, people need to experience the feeling of connectedness, to feel as if an invisible thread exists connecting them with the other person. There are several ways that such contact can be demonstrated in any interaction: through *eye contact*; through *short verbal phrases* such as "uh huh" and "I see" that indicate we have heard what the other person is saying; and through *non-verbal behaviors* such as head nods or other gestures that demonstrate we are following the gist of what the other person is saying.

The impact of *eye contact* is immediate in making positive contact. Eye contact indicates involvement. When people use eye contact it is as if they are saying, "I'm home" or "You've gotten my attention." Eye contact provides a symbolic connection.

Not everyone is comfortable with eye contact. Some people have difficulty using it. Early training has a lot to do with individual differences. For instance, some children are told, "Always look at me when I'm talking to you." Others are instructed that respect and deference are shown to one's elders by averting the eyes. Eye contact is not synonymous with staring. It involves a combination of both looking at the other person and also looking away. Observe your comfort level with eye contact. Notice how others respond to various degrees of eye contact. If you are not comfortable with eye contact, practice using it. Practice will help put you more at ease.

We need to show people that we are attuned to what they are saying. Head *nods* signal that we are following the gist of a conversation. Being listened to and understood are important to people. Therefore we use the nods as one way to let them know we hear what they are saying and understand their feelings.

Head nods, of course, cannot be seen over the telephone, so in their place substitute appropriate grunts and verbal expressions. These include "uh huh," "check," "yup," "gotcha," and "I'm following," which can be included in face-to-face contact as well. The important thing is to let the other person know you are still tuned in to what they are saying. As a sender, be sure you are getting the appropriate signals from your listeners. If not, it is wise to check in with them to be certain that they are listening and understand what they hear.

Thorough

Thoroughness is a theme of *The Upset Book*. One cause of upset in other people is their belief that they have been short-changed in some way. An easy way to prevent upset in other people is to be thorough in our dealings with them. If we are thorough, there is less opportunity for something to go wrong. The added bonus in thoroughness is the response of other people. Once they see that we are attending to them with care and in detail, they are less likely to respond with upset, anger or hurt.

Forward

Chapter One described the natural tendency to want to run the other way when someone is approaching angrily or upset. Similarly, if we have made a mistake, our inclination is to want to keep it a secret. The "F" for *forward* signifies that making positive contact requires us to come forward, particularly at those times when a back door exit would feel like the perfect escape. For example, an angry customer prefers the salesperson who moves quickly forward and says, "You seem upset about something. Can I be of help?" The customer is likely to relax because it appears that someone actually wants to assist in the resolution of the problem. The salesperson who comes forward is in direct contrast to the one who, because of discomfort in dealing with upset, ignores the customer's upset. The customer then ends up with initial (primary) upset and added dismay at being ignored (secondary upset).

When I (Pennie) was a child, curiosity compelled
me to completely disassemble my mother's
watch, which had been a tenth anniversary gift
from my father. I may have been adept at taking
the watch apart but I was totally incapable of
reversing the process. In dismay and fear I
disposed of the evidence. In so doing, I quickly
learned that I had more than doubled my
trouble. I was confronted with a mother who
was not only upset because I had taken her
watch apart but who was absolutely beside
herself because I had thrown it away. Both she
and I wished that I had come forward after the
first indiscretion and confessed my crime.

We have wondered for years about the "chicken or egg"
effect at seminars we teach. Those who sit toward the
front of the room seem to enjoy the seminar more and get
more from it than those who fill up the most distant
seats. Do those who sit toward the front already have a
more positive attitude or does coming forward help to
make experiences more meaningful?

We believe that moving forward pays dividends in our
personal lives, professional lives and in social and
commercial situations. Coming forward when we have
made mistakes or are faced with an unpleasant situation
has fewer repercussions than avoidance or escape.
Coming forward to partake of life's experiences adds
richness to our world.

Understand

All people appreciate being understood and are much
less likely to become upset if they feel they are
approached with understanding. When we understand

other people, we are making positive contact with them. Understanding other people is valuable in preventing upset and equally valuable in managing situations where people are already upset. In order to understand other people, it is necessary to be open to what they have to say. We need to be *willing* to communicate openly with others and also to *show* our openness. There is little room for a critical, evaluative mind-set in dealing with people.

Listen

Listening sounds like an easy behavior, yet it is one of the most difficult. We have all had the experience of talking to someone who is pretending to listen. We rarely are fooled. We know the difference between really being heard and a faked listening response. Good listening has prevented much potential upset. Listening and understanding will be more fully discussed in Chapters Seven and Eight.

Activities For T-A-C-T-F-U-L

A few activities are listed in this section to help you develop the ability to make positive contact. As has been indicated, approaching people and responding to them is an acquired skill. Our everyday interactions with people are the most effective activity for developing positive contact skills. The following activities can be practiced in your daily life.

1) At business and social gatherings practice approaching people you don't know with the idea of learning about them. Avoid talking only to those people you already know. Use TACTFUL.

2) Take opportunities to introduce yourself to people you don't know. Smile, extend your hand, identify yourself and say, "I don't believe we've met before."

3) If you think someone is upset, check this out with him or her at the earliest opportunity. "You seem upset. Is something bothering you?" Come forward rather than avoid a potential issue.

4) Ask co-workers, family or friends for feedback about your style. Do they feel you are listening and connected? Do they think you are open to what they are saying? Do your nonverbal gestures indicate you are following what they are saying? You can make copies of the shyness inventory and the personal communication inventory and ask family members, coworkers or friends to fill them out about you.

5) Practice observing people. Look for qualities you like and admire. Do not focus on people's flaws. Practice sharing something positive. Keep written lists of qualities you like in other people. Practice writing a note or memo of appreciation.

In addition to the TACTFUL elements, there are at least three other elements involved in making positive contact.

Remembering Names

A person's name is his or her own unique, personal label. Learning, remembering and being able to use a person's name is very important in making positive contact.

We can learn a person's name in several ways. They can

tell us. We can ask. We can learn it by observing it on a credit card, their records or other paper work. We can learn it by being told by someone else. Those of us who want to make a good positive connection with someone will be certain to take the time and trouble to learn the name.

> Mr. L. frequently bumped into us at community functions. Since he never seemed to remember our names, we always reintroduced ourselves. In a moment of extreme honesty, Mr. L. said, "I'm terrible at names but to tell you the truth, I never remember names 'cause I never really hear them in the first place."

Like Mr. L., some of you may be saying, "I can never remember peoples' names." And like Mr. L., the most common reason for being unable to remember a name is that we haven't really heard it and learned it in the first place. So, the first key to remembering a name is to listen to it carefully. Then use it. Repeat it. If it's a difficult or foreign name, continue trying to pronounce it correctly until you and the person whose name you are learning are satisfied. If you can immediately use a name three times after learning it, you will be more successful at remembering it. When you meet many people at one time, there is less expectation that you will remember everyone's name. But follow the above suggestions and you will be surprised at how many names you can learn at a time.

Once you have the name in your repertoire, by all means use it. As you talk to people, appropriately punctuate your conversation with their names. It personalizes the interactions. People feel unique and special. Later, when we talk about the specifics of dealing with very angry or upset people, we will again talk about the importance of names. Staying angry is more difficult when you are not anonymous.

One of the frequently asked questions about names is when to use first and last names. The setting, the age of the parties involved and the nature of the interaction all play a role in such a decision. A good rule of thumb, however, is that when in doubt, it is safer to be more formal. It is much easier for a person to request, "Call me Tom," than it is for him to say, "I prefer to be called Mr. Smith."

A corollary question about names is, "When is it appropriate to use Mrs., Ms., or Miss?" Fortunately, this question is becoming increasingly easier to answer as the use of Ms. becomes more and more acceptable. Good judgment is invaluable. If, for example, you are interacting with a 78-year-old woman wearing a wedding band, you are reasonably safe using Mrs. With most young women, Ms. is the appropriate choice.

A closing point of information. Anytime you forget someone's name don't be afraid to ask again. Asking says you care enough to seek it.

Free Information

The more quickly you learn about another person, the more able you are to tailor your interactions specifically to them. The quicker you gain information about another, the more readily positive contact can be cemented. Free information is information people share about themselves without being asked. They do this in several ways. Sometimes they simply tell us. In the course of talking, others share bits and pieces of information about themselves and their lives.

Margaret needed help in her business but had only enough money to hire someone for a half-time position. At a community meeting, she met Ted who mentioned that he would be taking early retirement the following month. He also mentioned his work history which included experience that might be applicable to the position Margaret needed to fill. The next day Margaret contacted Ted. A part-time position was very appealing to him. It would allow him to make a transition into retirement. The free information was probably responsible for Ted being offered the job and for the solution to Margaret's dilemma.

Sometimes free information is available on Channel Five, the channel of symbolic communication. For example, if someone has pictures of children and grandchildren in their office and home, it is a statement of what's important to him or her. A person who dresses fashionably is sending a message different from the person who dresses casually or conservatively. Homes or offices that are neat as pins, are filled with art, house plants or sports memorabilia each give us a lot of free information about the person who lives or works there. Even a person's car is a symbolic statement about him or her. Good powers of observation are invaluable tools. Utilizing free information as we deal with others helps us personalize our interactions.

Personalizing

Using names and free information is part of a larger process called personalizing. Positive contact involves personalizing. Personalizing is custom tailoring to other people what we say and do to fit the people with whom we are talking. It lets people know that we are aware of their individuality. It includes all the little touches that help the other person know we see them as important, as unique and as worthy of our time and effort.

Activities For Remembering Names,

Free Information and Personalizing

1) When you meet someone new, listen carefully to their name. If necessary, ask them to repeat it, help you pronounce it or spell it. Use their name at least three times, even if the interaction is brief. Do this whenever you are meeting someone new.

2) When you are with people, be aware of things they tell you about themselves, other people or their situation that you did not ask about. Are there parts of the free information you are filing away? Can you think of ways to use the information that might be helpful to you and the other person?

3) Select one or two people on whom to practice personalizing skills. Keep the focus on the other person. Ask questions and share information that uniquely addresses the person's interests. Use their name frequently in the conversation. Observe their channels of communication in order to get a reading of how they are experiencing the interaction.

We have described the art of making positive contact — the style of interacting that prevents people from upset. Positive contact is useful in establishing relationships, in maintaining good relationships and in preventing secondary upset.

CHAPTER SIX
COMPLAINTS

SIX

The telephone complaints began shortly after mail had been delivered in the western Kansas community. The local rural electric company was swamped with calls about the month's electric bill. The number of complaints were so high that the billing department decided to check out the situation. It only took a few minutes before it was discovered that a computer error had doubled the figure for everyone's monthly statement.

The above story illustrates several points about complaints we will be making in this chapter. As we shift to discussing some specific strategies for handling upset people, we well begin by talking about those people who complain, worry or get upset because they lack the ability to problem solve effectively. We believe it is easier to respond to complaints when we understand what they mean.

In the remaining chapters, we will be talking about dealing with greater amounts of frustration, upset, anger, grief and loss.

Complaints

What are complaints? The better we understand exactly what complaints are, the easier it will be to handle upset people who are complaining. Once we understand what complaints are, we are less likely to feel so personally attacked by them. First of all a **complaint is information**. It is feedback to us about something. The customer, the patient, the employee, the family member who complains to us is giving us information about a situation and telling us they value the relationship with us enough to want to work things out. Complaints tell us that the complaining person wishes to continue to interact with us. Where there are no complaints, there are no opportunities for improvement. We rarely hear the complaint of the person who has decided to stop doing business with us, to leave his or her job or to leave a personal relationship.

> An elderly man came home one night and told his wife of thirty-six years that he had filed for divorce. Absolutely every detail of the divorce had already been planned and executed. The wife was dumbfounded. She had no idea that her husband was so unhappy. Had he complained more and sooner, changes might have been made to help make the marriage more satisfactory for both husband and wife. He left the marriage and with him left any opportunity this couple may have had to improve their relationship.

Secondly and most importantly, **a complaint is a gap between a person's expectation and his or her experience.** If we expect employees to arrive at work at 8:00 and they arrive at 8:00, there is no gap between the expectation and the experience and therefore there is no complaint. On the other hand, we complain about the employee who is thirty minutes late for work — arriving at 8:30 when we expected him or her at 8:00. If we expect our call to be returned within the hour and it is not, we complain. If we are told the person we are calling is out of town for three days, we are not upset when they don't return the call within the hour.

> One evening two couples who had seen a terrible movie were discussing it over dessert and coffee. Three of the four people were complaining about the story line, the acting and how slow the film moved. At that point the fourth person said: "I only agreed to go to this movie because the rest of you wanted to see it. I wasn't at all disappointed with it because I never expected to like it in the first place."

How do expectations develop in the first place? Expectations are established in at least five different ways. They can be the result of *projecting* expectations about our own behavior to other people. If, for example, we always put our dirty clothes in the hamper and hang up the clothing we wore today, we will complain when another member of our household leaves things lying about.

Expectations are also formed by *past experience.* The patient who was last hospitalized twenty years ago may expect the current hospital bill to be much lower than it is because they are still thinking of health care costs as they were two decades ago. The couple married eight years may complain if they continue to expect their sexual relationship to have the same level of excitement and wonderment it had when they first discovered each other. Employers may complain about employees who were working fifty hours a week to complete a special project but who now are working forty hours a week as contracted.

Our expectations can develop out of some *previous experience* with a person or an organization. The physician who has always been timely in keeping appointments is more likely to receive a complaint when running late than the physician who historically is always 20 minutes behind schedule.

The *media* has some responsibility for the formation of our expectations. When an insurance ad shows claims people handing out checks at disaster scenes, we are more likely to complain if it takes our insurance company several weeks to get a check to us after an accident or a burglary. Likewise, we may complain when our family problems are not easily resolved because on television all family problems seem to get resolved in either thirty or sixty minutes.

Other people affect our expectations. If our friend's spouse does all the grocery shopping and cooking, then we are more likely to expect it of our spouse. If several people at work report that their doctors will see them after working hours, then we are more likely to expect late hours from our own physician. If our friends have secretaries who pay their personal bills, we may begin to expect the same from our secretary. If our neighbors report that their insurance companies put new roofs on their houses after the last storm, then we are more likely to expect the same from our insurance company.

Finally, a major source of expectations are our *wishes, hopes* and *fears.* If we are told that our broken leg should mend in six to eight weeks, our hopes and wishes will have us expect to be out of the cast within six weeks —

any time more than that will be the likely cause of complaints and additional upset. Similarly, if we are afraid that the appliance store will refuse to give us credit or replace our new, but unsatisfactory, television set, we may approach that store complaining and angry based on that fear induced expectation.

Given, then, that complaints are gaps between people's expectations and their experience, we can reduce complaints in two ways. First of all, we can try to help people set realistic expectations. We're better off telling someone it will take six weeks to receive a check than to say four to six weeks and have the person disappointed and complaining when the check arrives in five weeks. Our natural tendency is to set expectations on the short end of the possibility, erroneously thinking we will get fewer complaints that way. In reality it's far better to have someone pleasantly surprised when an expectation is exceeded than disappointed because the experience did not live up to the expectation.

Secondly, we can work to make an experience match an expectation as closely as possible. This means either matching the standard that is expected or coming forward and announcing a different standard. For example, we need either to arrive home by the time we have said we would or to call home and announce we'll be late.

Last but not least, **complaints are opportunities** — opportunities to change people's expectations and experiences so that future complaints can be reduced.

Chronic Complainers

The world is full of people who might best be described as chronically upset about something. Chronic complainers are one example of the chronically upset. Chronic complainers are people who always complain about something. People chronically complain for many different reasons. A few of those reasons are listed below.

- They learned to complain because it was the behavioral style of the family in which they grew up.

- They were reinforced in some way for complaining (remember the manipulative child described in Chapter Three).

- They haven't discovered a way to get other people to listen to them and take them seriously.

- They are pleading for attention in the only way they know how.

Harry had moved from Houston a year earlier to a town about 100 miles from Chicago. Harry's widowered father lived in Chicago. After the move, Harry began receiving frequent and frantic calls from his father. These calls were filled with complaints about various health problems. Weekends had Harry making hurried trips to Chicago in response to his father's upsetting calls. Within six months, Harry found himself overwhelmed by his father's health complaints. He also began hearing a new set of complaints from his wife, who resented Harry spending all of his weekends with his father in Chicago.

Meeting the demands associated with chronic complaints is not usually the solution to eliminating the problem. Here is what we suggest.

The first step in dealing with the chronic complainer is listening. We must fight the natural tendency to stop listening when dealing with the chronic complainer. We listen in order to understand the purpose of the complaining. In Harry's case his Dad may have been saying, "I'm lonely" or "I'd like to see you." If so, Harry can respond to the true meaning of the complaint. For example, he might try calling his Dad more frequently and just chatting. Or he could say, "I know you wish I could come to Chicago this weekend but that won't be possible. Mildred and I can come up the weekend of August 16th if that will work with your schedule." In this way, Harry would have more control over the scheduling of his visits. Or, he might say, "When you are feeling better, I'll try to get to Chicago so that we can spend a couple of hours together. I'd hate to waste a trip when you're not feeling well enough to visit or do anything." This response helps Harry's Dad to change his behavior (complain less) if he wants to spend time with Harry. When we respond immediately to inappropriate complaints and requests, we are teaching complainers to continue to complain. By listening carefully, we can learn to hear the problem underlying the complaint. Then we can focus on teaching the complainer a new and more functional method for getting his or her needs met.

Chronic complaining sometimes results in complainers feeling so overwhelmed by their problems that they then overwhelm us with their complaints. A useful technique for handling this kind of upset is what we call *making molehills out of mountains*. Big problems can be overwhelming! Renovating an old house, for example, is a monumental task. Tackling one room at a time subdivides the goal in such a way as to allow the experience of success at shorter intervals. It is easier to focus on the house one room at a time. When dealing with an upset person who is feeling swamped by the problem, help him or her to break it down into manageable chunks.

To further illustrate this point, let's imagine someone has been complaining to you that his spouse or his boss finds fault with everything he does. Such accusations may feel mountainous to him. After listening attentively, ask this person to focus on just one of the things about which his wife or boss is unhappy — something he, too, would like to change. If, for example, he responds that both he and his wife wish he could be neater, he still is in danger of continuing to feel overwhelmed by that problem alone. We can help him by asking him to identify one household task related to neatness that he thinks he could manage to accomplish in the next week. The goal is to help the upset person work on a problem that has high likelihood of turning out successfully.

Just as individuals can feel overwhelmed by their problems, so can whole families or whole organizations feel overwhelmed by problems. Turning mountains into molehills is one way to directly attack this kind of upset.

Finally, some people become chronic complainers about

chronic complainers. If you find yourself surrounded by upset people who continually complain to you, you are in danger of becoming a complainer about complainers. It may be time for you to assert yourself and state your limits. You may need to say such things as:

- "I'm sorry but I can't listen any more."

- "Unless you really want to work on changing the problem, it doesn't feel fruitful to continue to talk about this."

- "If you can't control your complaining about this, we will be spending less time together."

Confronting people in order to help them to help themselves can be helpful for both parties. It is better to state your limits than it is to withdraw, leaving the chronic complainer to ponder the reason for your withdrawal (and, no doubt, the withdrawal of others).

In addition to chronic complainers, there are some other categories of chronically upset people that most of us find difficult. Let's look at a few kinds of chronic upset and discuss strategies for coping with them.

Chronic Worriers

Whereas chronic complainers are upset about present issues, chronic worriers are upset about the possibility of a future problem, the "what ifs." Worrying originates from long-term habit or from a superstitious belief that through worry, one can control the future. Chronic worriers believe that if they give up worrying, they would increase the possibility of their fears coming true. Since worry consumes a great deal of time, giving up worrying would also present chronic worriers with the potential problem of how to fill time previously spent worrying. The following list provides some tips for managing the upset of the chronic worrier.

- Help worriers to turn their worry into planning. Use questions like:

  "If that happened, what would you do?"

  "What, in your worry, can you control? How likely is that to occur?"

  "What would happen if that occurred?"

- Don't dismiss the concerns of the worrier with statements such as "don't be silly."

- Make rational input such as described in Chapter Four.

- Help worriers to restructure their worry. For example, they might keep a worry log or diary to help them get a sense of the scope of their worry. Or they might set aside a certain time of the day for worrying and save all their worries until that special time.

Worriers can also make a list of their worries. The list can help them to sort out:

- Worries they cannot control such as: "What if it rains on the day of the Sunday School picnic? Since they cannot control the weather, worry will not help. But planning will help.

- Worries they can plan for such as: "What will we do if it rains on the day of the Sunday School picnic?" This is the list that worriers really can tackle.

- Worries that are irrational and therefore highly unlikely to happen such as: "What if it rains the day of the Sunday School picnic and after holding the picnic in the community hall of the church, a tornado blows the church away?" The worrier can calculate the odds of such a happening and then decide how much energy to put into worrying. In addition, worriers could plan for those aspects of the worry that planning would help. For example, if there was a very bad storm, what would we need to do?

My Problems Are My Friends

Another category of chronically upset people are those whose longstanding problems have become such familiar companions that they would feel lost without them. "What would I focus on without my problem?" is part of what maintains the problem. The old behaviors that are causing problems have become habits. Despite the fact that the problems are upsetting, it would be hard to know how to act without them. Alcohol counselors recognize that alcoholics need to change their lives in order to overcome their addiction. Likewise, spouses of alcoholics also have to change their lives when the alcoholic stops drinking. They need to learn new roles and behaviors if they are to be successful as the spouse of a nondrinking person. If they have been spending their time being the all-responsible member of the family and their spouse stops drinking and is now able to help share the responsibility, they may need to find new activities to fill time previously spent on family chores. Otherwise, there is always the risk that they will unknowingly sabotage the new sober behavior. The person chronically upset over a problem that has become an old friend needs help in grieving the loss that change precipitates. All change, even hoped for change, involves loss. We will be discussing how best to help people cope with loss in Chapter Nine.

In addition to grieving their loss, people who constantly complain about a problem may need help learning new roles and behaviors if they are to be divested of their problem. For example, if the daughter of a bedridden parent has received praise for "being such a good daughter," she may need help finding new roles through which to maintain her sense of value once she no longer has responsibility for her parent. Less time spent on caretaking would require new interests and activities to replace the behaviors that were involved in caring for the aging parent.

Unrealistic Expectations

Some people suffer from holding chronically unrealistic expectations which then are responsible for their becoming or staying upset. Expectations can be too high, too low or they may not match the situation. For example, some parents expect their children always to perform at a very high level. Other parents, frankly, don't care much if their children accomplish anything at all. And some parents place the same expectations on all of their children, never taking into account their different skills and abilities. Each set of expectations involves the potential for disappointment and upset.

Unsolvable Problems

Defining a problem in such a way that it is unsolvable is another way in which people maintain or escalate their upset.

- "The problem is I'm getting old."
- "The problem is I'm a woman/man/ black/short/tall etc."
- "The problem is my mother never loved me."

Such problems truly are not solvable. When faced with an unsolvable problem, check to see if there is another way to describe it. Rational self-talk, as discussed in Chapter Four, can help to redefine problems in ways that permit solutions. People are less upset when they feel their problems can be solved. When we can take action, we are less likely to feel helpless and hopeless. The unsolvable problems described above can be restated:

- "The problem is my reaction to aging. How can I change my reaction?"
- "The problem is how to hurdle some of the barriers related to who I am."
- "The problem is how to get my needs met now."

Once problems are defined in such ways that solutions are possible, upset is lessened because people can begin looking for solutions.

> Elaine, a bright, attractive woman in her forties, was devastated when her job of twenty-one years was terminated. She sadly announced, "I'll never find another job as good as this one."

When pressed for evidence that she was indeed unlikely to find another good job, Elaine's examples included that she was too old; too particular; too perfectionistic, and too organized. She seemed surprised when a friend imagined a scene in which a company would value her experience and those skills. Looking at the problem in this new way changed Elaine's problem to one of finding a position which would utilize what she had to offer. If Elaine should choose to redefine the problem as "How can I learn to relax some of my perfectionistic standards?" then the solution will lie in her learning some new behaviors.

Upset Created By Errors In Problem Solving

Upset can escalate when people lack appropriate problem-solving skills. Often, in our counseling practice, couples and families arrive for counseling feeling very upset about the number and magnitude their problems. The upset they describe is not related to one specific problem. They have many problems because they have not developed skills for working out solutions. We all have and will always have some problems to face. The ability to cope with our problems and find workable solutions to them is the key to dealing with upset resulting from problems. A number of frequently made mistakes in problem solving follows:

Moving to Problem-Solving Too Quickly

In a previous chapter we described the importance to the upset person of expressing feelings. What is most needed in upset is a "caring parent" to listen to the "upset child." Even when the upset person has a problem to solve, sharing what is truly troubling him or her may take some time. In solving the first problem the upset person describes, we might be solving the wrong problem. The critical point here is be patient — don't move too quickly to problem solving.

Getting Married to One Solution

Most decisions are *not* chipped in stone. Upset is sometimes related to a belief that once we make a decision, we are forever stuck with it. On the contrary, it is frequently possible to change our minds.

> A young man about to graduate from high school informed his parents that he had no interest in going on to college. He preferred to look for a job. His parents, recognizing that he was bright enough to attend college, tried to insist that college was his only possible choice. Everyone's upset was considerable until the boy's father suggested that the boy try college for one semester. The young man did not have to feel trapped into a choice that might not work and the parents did not have to feel that their son had totally avoided a possible option. Neither parents nor son had to stay married to only one solution.

Limited Search for Alternatives

This mistake in the problem-solving process is closely related to the one above. Sometimes it feels like there will be relief in a quick and easy "fix." But taking the time to brainstorm can be an important part of the process. For most kinds of upset, many alternative solutions are possible. Don't limit your search for alternatives. Your imagination can sometimes lead you to a creative solution to a problem. Looking at many possible solutions improves the odds that we will select a good one. Then the upset person can feel more assured that the solution is a good one.

Looking for Saviors

Upset people sometimes think that some one thing is going to be the answer to the problem or to all their problems.

"If only I had more money."

"If I could just get married."

"Moving would solve all my problems."

Solutions in the form of seeking saviors are rarely satisfactory for the long term. The key to the long range management of upset is the development of sound coping skills. We will always have problems. But we can learn a process for handling them. Coping skills are built on a variety of foundations. Examples of these include the practice of problem solving behaviors or an appropriate reliance on religious faith.

Analysis Paralysis

Some of us tend to spend too much time and energy analyzing problems that don't warrant such detailed attention. Decisions such as what to wear, what to cook for dinner, whether to sell the family business or whether to leave one's spouse are not all of equal importance. If we worry as much about what to wear as we do about whether or not to divorce, we are likely to be perpetually upset. In dealing with the upset person who is prone to over analysis, several techniques can be helpful.

- Ask, "What's the worse thing that can happen?" For example, "What's the worst that could happen if you proposed your idea at the meeting?"

- Use humor and over exaggeration. "So, you're afraid if you stated your ideas the entire group would run screaming from the room. What a great way to shorten the meeting!"

- Use assertive straight-talk. Let them know that you think they need to lighten up. "I'm concerned about you. You seem overwhelmed by the prospect of presenting your ideas. You are a valuable member of the group and your participation is expected."

Lack of Implementation

Problem solving needs to result in the implementation of a proposed solution. It is not enough to think of a solution. We have to use the solution after we have developed it. Longstanding or continued upset is sometimes the product of lack of implementation. Committee meetings can often be examples of the problem of lack of implementation. Everyone has ideas and suggestions but no one wants to carry them out.

Teach Them to Fish

To help and to take over are not the same thing. Problems of upset people are not solved by feeling sorry for the person or feeling the need to take over for them.

On the contrary, we are successful in dealing with upset people when we help them get a sense of their own power in a situation. We accomplish this by being in charge of ourselves and by *not* taking over for the upset person.

> After the grief of her husband's death subsided, one of my (Don's) grandmother's most pressing problems was how to get herself around town since she didn't know how to drive. My mother did both of them a favor. She provided the money for driving lessons. Despite being over seventy years old, Grandmother mastered driving. It was marvelous for her sense of accomplishment. And my mother never had to feel angry or resentful about being tied down as Grandmother's chauffeur.

Hopefully this chapter has helped you to change how you talk to yourself about complaints and given you some understanding as to how to respond to chronic complainers, worriers and ineffective problem solvers. Now, let's turn our attention to dealing with upset people.

■

CHAPTER SEVEN
DEALING WITH UPSET PEOPLE

SEVEN

Ben's mother knew that whenever Ben asked for hot chocolate, it meant he was upset about something. She'd carefully prepare the hot chocolate, after which the two of them would sit down together, sipping the cocoa and talking. What usually happened was that Ben talked about what was bothering him while his mother listened attentively. Sometimes Ben's problem got solved. Sometimes it didn't. Often Ben forgot to drink his hot chocolate. But the ritual always helped him to feel better.

Those of us who have had the good fortune to be listened to attentively when we are feeling upset understand the relief Ben experienced from the warmth of his mother's listening. Those of us who have had our feelings ignored, mocked or dismissed understand the frustration of unsoothed upset. The principles which Ben's mother used in responding to his upset can be applied to dealing with upset people in general.

Most of us find ourselves face-to-face with upset people. The need to deal with upset people exists even when we have used all the principles of positive contact. The following formula provides the basic recipe for dealing with people who are upset.

The Formula For Dealing With Upset People

There are five ingredients in the formula for dealing with upset people. These are: listening, empathizing, clarifying, problem solving and closing. After we describe and discuss each ingredient, we will provide some practice exercises that are designed to help you increase your skills in dealing with upset people.

Listening

Good listening is easier said than done. It takes skill and practice. It requires giving total attention to the other person. Listening involves carefully scanning the other person's seven communication channels. When we practice listening, we pay attention to all the messages the other person sends and we do so until they are finished speaking. While such intense attention may sound time consuming, it saves time in the long run. People who are upset demand to be heard. Not listening to upset people makes them even more determined to describe their problem. When we listen well, the upset person doesn't need to spend unnecessary time capturing our attention. In addition, good listening communicates caring.

In order to listen well, we need to pay special attention to the language channel. Information presented on the language channel provides us with the facts about the upset. We also need to be tuned into the channel that carries feelings. The feeling channel helps us gain an understanding of what the upset person is feeling. As a rule of thumb, the more upset people are, the less they are likely to share on the language channel and the more they will provide on the feeling channel.

Since upset people are generally behaving out of their child ego state, they respond best to caring parents. Unfortunately, some of us are more likely to respond as critical parents than as caring parents when dealing with the upset person's child ego state. Most of us have spent long years developing the ability to listen for those things with which we disagree. When we argue with others, our ears seem trained to listen for and point out the holes in their thinking. The other person may have spoken for several minutes and said several things with which we have no argument. But the moment something is said with which we don't agree, it is almost like we are saying, "Aha, I caught you." Success in dealing with upset people requires *listening for agreement*. To agree with another person on some points greatly reduces friction and upset.

In summary, there are three basic ideas to remember and practice when listening to upset people:

- listen attentively to the whole story from beginning to end
- listen for understanding of feelings as well as of issues
- listen for areas of agreement

Activities for Developing Listening Skills

1) Listen carefully to a television news cast or to a religious broadcast. Listen for:
   - content

- feelings

- agreement

Note the differences in your response when you personally agree or disagree with it.

2) Ask a friend to help you with this exercise. Have your friend share something about which he or she is or has been upset — perhaps an issue with a spouse, boss, child or another friend; perhaps a complaint about something annoying. Listen carefully for both the content and the feelings. Then rephrase what you think the person was saying and feeling. Ask your friend for feedback as to how you did. If necessary, continue to refine your rephrasing of the content and understanding of the feelings. Do not get caught up in trying to "fix" your friend's complaint. Just listen for understanding.

Empathizing

Empathy is defined as the ability to put oneself in another person's shoes; the mental ability to identify oneself with another person. When we successfully empathize with someone, we are making appropriate use of our caring parent ego state.

One way to describe empathy is to describe what it is not. Empathy is *not* minimizing the problem. It is *not* saying, "That's not so bad" or "It could be worse." Nor is it saying, "Oh my gosh, that's awful." Empathy is *not* advice. It is *not* telling someone how to solve a problem. And finally, empathy is *not* taking the attention off the upset person and redirecting it to oneself. This is not helpful. In hospital settings, for example, a visitor sometimes attempts to cheer a patient by describing personal illnesses, surgeries and health issues. The poor upset, ill and captive patient! Empathy is *not* saying, "So you think *you've* got a problem."

To empathize *is* to listen to another person's complaint or upset feelings without making judgments. The more we experience the other person's viewpoint, the easier it is to empathize. We need to be able to identify with the feelings of a child when he or she is being teased by playmates; a roommate who is fighting with the friend; a family member who is upset because we are two hours late arriving home; an employee who feels overwhelmed by a task. When we can put ourselves in other people's shoes, we can better understand their upset.

What are some of the things that get in the way of our ability to empathize? There are at least four.

Feeling Attacked

Feeling personally attacked can limit our capacity to empathize. When we feel we are being personally attacked, the natural, instinctive response is to mobilize to defend ourselves. We defend rather than listen and empathize. In a later chapter we will provide you with some self-management techniques that can help you overcome these defensive feelings.

Fear of Responsibility

A second factor that can interfere with our ability to empathize with and understand others is our fear that we may be responsible for the upset in some way. To empathize with someone is not the same thing as admitting fault. It is possible to express concern without taking responsibility. We are not suggesting that each of us doesn't sometimes bear some responsibility for another person's upset. It is important, however, to have sufficient information about a problem before rushing in and admitting fault. Below are some statements of problems and several pairs of responses to each problem. Both responses express understanding and concern. One of the responses, however, also takes on more responsibility or fault than is recommended based on available information. Take a few minutes to read through the following six pairs of examples and check the response you think is preferable. Remember, we are looking for ways to show concern without taking on responsibility.

1. "I just received your check from the bank marked 'insufficient funds'."

   A. "If there's a problem, I certainly want to correct it."

   B. I'm not usually overdrawn."

2. "Your daughter was very rude to me when I called."

   A. "I'm embarrassed she was rude. I've tried to teach her good manners."

   B. "I'm sorry you were upset. How can I help you?"

3. "You never listen to anything I say."

A. "I know it can be upsetting to feel ignored. What would you like me to listen to now?"

B. "You're right. I get caught up in my own thoughts too much."

4. "Where are the reports for tomorrow's meeting? You were supposed to have them here by now."

   A. "I'll be there with them in an hour. It would concern me if things didn't run smoothly."

   B. "I'm sorry the reports are late."

5. "My wife slipped on your steps yesterday and her back is giving her a lot of trouble today."

   A. "We really need new carpeting on those steps."

   B. "I hope your wife is taking care of her back."

6. "You people sent the wrong order to us. It arrived this morning."

   A. "I'm sorry if it wasn't what you expected."

   B. "I'm sorry! We are usually more careful."

The preferred responses are: 1-A; 2-B; 3-A; 4-A; 5-B; 6-A. You can practice developing concern without admitting liability by anticipating people's complaints and preparing in advance some responses to them.

Personal Insecurity

Insecurity about ourselves, our abilities, our families and anything else that is important to us can also affect our empathizing skills. The more secure a person feels, the easier it is to lower defenses, to listen and to empathize.

Limited Perspective

The ability to empathize can be obstructed by having a limited perspective about other people. How can we put ourselves in another person's shoes if we have not had any similar life experiences? If we've always been able to eat everything we wanted to eat without gaining weight, how can we understand what it's like to have a chronic weight problem? If we've always been employed, how can we understand the person who has been out of work? If we lack a frame of reference in which to place a situation, we will be less effective at empathizing.

However, never having experienced something doesn't necessarily mean we are unable to understand it. We can develop empathy around many situations by remembering similar experiences in our own lives and by imagining what it would feel like if we had the other person's problem. We may never have been unemployed, but we can try to imagine the feelings we would have if we had no place to go in the morning, no money coming in, no way to provide for our family and no sense of productivity. Using our imaginations is an excellent way of improving our ability to empathize with people.

Statement of Understanding

The opening comment in an empathy statement is a brief statement of understanding directed toward the other person's complaint or upset. "I understand you had a bad day." "I'm sorry you worried about my being late." "It's tough when you are having problems with an account." Each of these is a statement of understanding. You'll notice that blame is not assigned in any of these statements. You have neither said "I'm sorry your client is difficult" nor "You really should try to be more service oriented with your clients."

When possible, empathy can be more than just a brief statement of understanding. It can provide an opening in which to communicate your understanding of the other person's feelings. "I'm sorry you and your mother are having problems. It must be very frustrating when you are trying so hard to be a good daughter."

When people are upset about something, they need reassurance that their feelings have been acknowledged and understood. This is not the same as reassuring someone that his or her feelings are "right." Like listening, the power of empathy cannot be overestimated. Many times, the primary request of the upset person is to be understood. We can *always* listen and empathize, even in situations where we cannot meet additional wishes of the upset person. At the least, we can empathize with and understand a person's wish. "I sure understand how much you wish you did not need surgery."

A couple of years ago, I (Pennie) became more than a little disgruntled with the phone company. I was without service for almost a week. Every day when I called, an operator would tell me that service would be restored before 6 p.m. the next day. Finally, on the sixth day when my phone was still not in working order, I rushed next door to use my neighbor's phone, verbally attacking the first operator I reached. After raving and ranting, running out of breath and wearing thin my vocal chords, I stopped and said, "I don't know why I'm yelling at you. I'm sure you're not responsible for my problem." Graciously the operator said, "It's O.K. lady, if it feels good to yell, go ahead and yell. I don't mind listening."

Activities for Developing Empathizing Skills

1) Observe others when you are out shopping, eating or participating in a community event. Try to imagine people's lives based on the cues they send. Imagine how they live, where they work, what their relationships are like and how they feel about different things.

2) We all are involved with people. Whenever you are having a conversation with another person, try to put yourself in his or her shoes. Think about how you would feel were you the other person.

3) Listen and watch carefully for what you think others are feeling. Notice the little ways in which people let you know what their feelings are. Check to make sure you understand their feelings by saying:

It sounds like you feel_____.

I can understand how you feel when_____.

Are you feeling_____?

Can you share your feelings with me?

Clarifying

There are times when an upset person just needs a sympathetic ear — someone to listen and understand. Situations related to grief are examples of these times. Although listening and empathizing are necessary, they are not always sufficient. In many situations, upset people are looking for a solution to their problem. It is necessary to be clear about the nature of the problem if we are to be successful in helping to resolve it. The third step in this formula is the giving and getting of information in order to determine if there is a problem to be solved and in order to correctly identify the problem. Whereas empathizing is putting yourself in the other person's shoes, clarifying is the process through which *both* parties gain a better understanding of the situation. In order to be helpful, we need to have full knowledge of the upset person's feelings and full knowledge of the content of the problem.

It may help to know what clarifying *is not* in order to better recognize what it *is*. Clarifying definitely is *not* evaluating, moralizing, lecturing or preaching — a fact sometimes forgotten by the eager helper. It is not useful to become critical parents when dealing with an upset person no matter how obviously the upset person may have mismanaged a situation or an aspect of his or her life. Critical parents turn upset people into defensive children. The goal in dealing with upset people is to move people into their adult ego state. This phase employs the useful exchange of information. Below we describe five particular behaviors that are helpful in successful clarifying.

Information Gathering

A role we often play in the clarifying process is that of information seeker. We may need more information than we have if we are going to be able to effectively help the upset person. A review of helpful information-seeking skills follows:

1) Paraphrasing and checking for understanding:

Paraphrasing involves repeating our understanding of the *content of the message* in our own words. Checking for understanding involves describing what we think the other person is *feeling*. A clear understanding of both the content of the message and the upset person's feelings is necessary in the successful management of upset. If we respond to what we *think* another person is saying or feeling, we may be wrong. It is impossible to go wrong by paraphrasing and checking for understanding. The other person may say, "Yes, that's what I meant" or "Yes, that's how I feel," or he or she may say, "No, let me try to explain again." In either case, we have improved our understanding of the nature of the upset.

2) Open vs. closed questions:

Open questions encourage the respondent to give more than a one-word answer. Open questions are useful for gaining information and for allowing the upset or complaining person to express his or her feelings. Examples of open-ended questions are:

"How are you feeling about moving to Minnesota?"

"You seem dissatisfied with your performance appraisal. What were you hoping or expecting?"

"What seems to be the problem with our budget?"

"How haven't I been holding up my end of the family responsibilities?"

When you are clarifying, open questions give you more information than the following closed questions. Example of closed questions are:

"Do you dislike colder climates?"

"Were you expecting a bigger salary increase?"

"Are we overdrawn?"

"Have the meals been O.K.?"

As you can see, these closed questions provide much more limited information.

Closed questions encourage brief, specific answers and are useful if you need to elicit specific information. Requests for dates, times and numbers, as well as questions that can be answered "yes" or "no" are closed questions. Closed questions may be helpful when someone is very upset, is out of control or has been talking too long. Then, the goal is to help them calm down and gain control of themselves. At such times, closed questions can follow an empathy statement. "I'm sorry you had to wait for me. How long will it take us to get organized?"

3) What, when, where and how vs. why:

Questions that ask what, where, when and how have us seeking information that will be useful in problem solving. "What would you like for dinner tomorrow?" "Where are you thinking about vacationing?" "How can we reduce on expenses?" Questions that begin with "why," on the other hand, require explanations and tend to put the upset person on the defensive. When we ask a person why he or she did something, that person, looks for a way to convince us that there was a good reason for the behavior.

"How do you think you might earn the money to pay for your speeding ticket?" is a more appropriate question to ask a seventeen-year-old son than "Why were you going so fast?" In phrasing the question this way, the parent communicates disapproval but also understanding of the son's dilemma. In addition to serving a clarifying function, the question focuses on problem solving. We can understand his upset and still share our disapproval. "I know you're upset you got a ticket and I need you to know that I do not expect you to drive fast or recklessly. I love you and want you safe."

It is often the *way* in which questions are asked (the manner channel) rather than what questions are being asked (the language channel) that escalates or reduces the other person's upset. It is important to have your manner convey genuine concern. "What in the world do *you* have to complain about?" is not what we mean by a "what" question. The inappropriate use of sarcasm has upset many a person who started out with only a mild complaint.

Finally, we need to remember that an upsetting incident involves two parties. We are not the only ones who have some responsibility for clarifying the issues. Sometimes our efforts at asking questions produce silence or even more upset. If none of our clarifying questions appear to be helpful, we can ask the upset person to tell us what he or she needs. We can ask, for example, "What would be helpful to you?" This redirects some of the responsibility back to the upset person and returns us to our goals of listening, understanding and clarifying

Information Giving

Another way of clarifying the problem is by giving an upset person information. For example, when I (Don) rushed to the emergency room with my son who had just broken his arm and the admitting person began asking for insurance information, my upset escalated. My son's broken arm is a crisis for me even though it is not a crisis for the emergency room personnel. Adding clarifying information to the request would have reduced my upset. "Can I ask you for your insurance card? It will help us get your son's broken arm looked at more quickly."

There are other ways in which information giving is clarifying for an upset person. We overheard a woman in a grocery store complaining to the manager that the milk her son had just purchased was spoiled. She demanded that the manager take back the milk and give her a new half gallon. The manager politely and quietly informed the woman that the particular brand of milk she was returning was the house brand of another chain of supermarkets. Needless to say her behavior changed dramatically. The information was essential to the outcome. As in information seeking, the manner channel is critical in information giving.

The purpose of clarifying is to enable both parties to develop a clearer understanding of the problem or issue. Roles also may need clarifying. Sometimes we are not sure what part the upset person expects us to play in a situation. For example, if a loved one comes home after a bad day at work and complains about the job is he or she asking for an understanding listener, advice about how to handle the boss or support for leaving the job and looking for a new one? When dealing with an upset person, it is also important to know whether you are a part of the problem.

Activities for Developing Clarifying Skills

1) As you talk with other people, be aware of the frequency with which you use what, where, when, how and why questions and open/closed questions. Practice eliminating the why questions. Look for new ways to ask for information. Practice asking open questions when you want to help other people express themselves and/or you want lots of information. Practice asking closed questions when you want specific information; when you want to help the other person be brief; when you want to help the other person control feelings. If you are wanting more open communication with your family members or work colleagues, you will find the art of questioning invaluable.

2) While reading or watching TV be aware of what information you are missing and would like to have. Write down specific questions. Write down information you think would be helpful to share.

3) Paraphrasing content and checking for understanding of feelings are just as critical to clarification as they are to empathizing. Therefore, the empathizing activities also can be used to help develop clarification skills. Paraphrase what you think the other person is saying. Check for understanding by using empathizing activity #3.

4) When giving instructions, request that the other person repeat the instructions back to you before starting the task.

5) When asked to do any assignment make a list of additional information that would help you perform the task. Practice asking your clarifying questions before approaching those who might have the answers.

Problem Solving

After the problem has been clearly identified, solutions can be sought. Problem solving, as mentioned previously, does not include blaming. Blaming assigns the problem to someone whereas effective problem solving requires that the problem be out on the table in front of both parties. Both parties can work together to seek a satisfactory solution. You do not need the answers to the upset person's dilemma in order to be effective in helping to solve the problem. However, you do need some ideas about how to go about the task of finding the answers. Suppose, for example, a friend or co-worker comes to you with a family problem. A son is suddenly acting moody and doing poorly in school. This person is certain that drug and alcohol abuse are involved. This person keeps asking "What shall I do?" Rather than being overwhelmed by the task of solving the problem, you need have some ideas about where help might be available. You may be helpful to the upset parent by directing him or her to a physician, a local mental health association, alcoholics anonymous, a school counselor or even the local phone book.

Problem-solving abilities can be enhanced by imagination, fantasy and brainstorming. Use any or all of the following to increase the number of creative solutions to sticky problems.

- Think of every possible solution — even those that seem crazy or impossible. Don't evaluate until you've exhausted all possibilities.

- Think of ideal outcomes.

- Think of the worst possible things to do.

- Check out solutions other people have used.

    A young couple spent the better part of several weeks fighting over vacation plans. The two unresolved issues were whether to include children and what means of transportation they could afford. Mother didn't want to spend two weeks in the car with the children and Father wanted to include the children but couldn't figure out how to manage five plane fares on their vacation budget. The couple was stuck. Once they began to fantasize the ideal situation, they were able to design a vacation plan that pleased everyone. Mom and Dad drove to Florida, enjoying a week to themselves. The children spent the first week with their grandparents. Both grandparents and grandchildren profited from this special family time. The children then flew to Florida to meet their parents. The two youngest children flew home. The eleven-year-old son enjoyed the privilege of several days alone with his parents on the return trip.

Additional Problem Solving Strategies

It is better to tell people what we *can* do for them than what we *can't* do.telling your thirteen-year-old daughter, "You can have six girl friends over for a pajama party next weekend" is preferable to, "Absolutely no boy-girl parties." The simple skill of using "can do" improves the likelihood of reducing upset.

When it is not possible to meet someone's request, use the word *can't* rather than *won't*. Saying you won't do something indicates you could do it but refuse to do so. Saying you can't suggests it is not possible.

Sometimes it is helpful to ask an upset person what he or she would suggest you do. In other words, return the problem to the upset person. When an upset person becomes responsible for finding the solution, he or she often realizes your dilemma and perhaps even the unreasonableness of the request. The upset person is more likely to accept a solution if he or she has had a role in developing it. If the person continues to be unreasonable, his or her feelings probably have not been effectively addressed. In this case, it is necessary to return to the listening and empathizing stages of the formula. The upset person is not ready for an adult-to-adult transaction.

> When my (Pennie) children were teenagers, they were sometimes upset by the limits I placed on them related to their curfew. Often I would ask them to set their own curfews. Not surprisingly, they would set hours that were agreeable to both of us.

Most upset people want to know that everything possible is being done to resolve their problem. Listening, understanding and giving them our very best shot at problem-solving is how we demonstrate our willingness to respond to their complaints and upset.

Activity for Developing Problem Solving Skills

Before you embark on the following exercise be certain that you can *identify* the problem. Correct problem identification is essential. If the problem has more than one part, do the exercise for each part of the problem.

Once you have identified the problem, use the following procedure. This activity can be done individually or can involve several people.

  a) List all possible solutions to the problem. If appropriate, ask others to add to your list. In this stage of problem solving do not evaluate the potential solutions. List everything, even if you are aware of problems in the solutions.

  b) Cross unacceptable solutions off the list.

c) Arrange the remaining solutions in a prioritized order; starting with those you like best and ending with those you like least. This part of the process usually requires that participating problem-solvers are aware of the benefits and costs of each possible solution.

d) Select the top choice solution and implement it.

e) Evaluate the solution you have selected after an appropriate time. Decisions are more difficult when we believe that once we decide on a course of action we can never change our mind.

f) If the solution is not working or if it is not helping solve the problem, select another potential solution from your list.

Suppose, for example, your daughter is upset by the problem of what to do with her life after high school graduation. The above problem-solving process may prove helpful. The list of solutions could include everything she can think of from going to college, to getting various jobs, to joining the military, to lying around doing nothing for a year. Don't forget to have her include even the most absurd possibilities. After eliminating unacceptable options and listing the remaining solutions based on the costs and benefits, she can select a course of action. Choosing one of the options will be easier if she limits herself to a particular time frame. She might decide, for example, "I will take a one-year electrician's training course at the local voca-tional/technical school. However, at the end of six months, I will evaluate how the course is working for me. If I discover I have little aptitude for or interest in, becoming an electrician, I will go back to my potential solutions list." Surprisingly, the freedom not to have to stick with an unsatisfactory choice often allows us to try new behaviors and, in the process, to discover new and exciting things.

If you are having difficulty making a decision related to a problem, try the following. Imagine the craziest, wildest, most ridiculous solution possible. What , if any, would be the value in such a wild, crazy solution? What would be some of the problems? The goal of this type of problem-solving activity is to help you let your imagination grow in order to be able to generate more creative solutions. We often learn that solutions we thought of as crazy are very workable.

> A woman was complaining about her husband's depression, particularly his lack of energy, his moodiness and his inability to make decisions. She said she had tried absolutely everything she could think of to help him snap out of it. When she was asked to think of the worst possible thing she could do with him, she thought for several pensive moments. Then she got a light bulb expression in her eyes, broke into a grin and said, "I thought of something awful I could do, but now that I think of it perhaps instead of being awful it's the one thing I should have been doing all along but have been too afraid to try. I think I need to confront him more directly about his behavior rather than just tippy-toe around him for fear I'll upset him. Maybe my tippy-toeing has sent him the message that he is truly fragile and unable to do much."

Problems Encountered in Problem Solving

It is not unusual for upset to be the result of the frustration we feel as we work at solving our everyday problems. Each of us approaches problem solving in a unique way. Some styles work better than others to lessen the frustration.

> In a restroom in the Los Angeles airport, a woman was attempting to obtain some soap from the soap dispenser. Over and over again, she pushed *up* on the lever of the soap dispenser. When nothing happened, she would redouble her attack on the wall-mounted bottle. The sign on the soap dispenser above another sink read "push *back* on handle." In that one brief moment, the woman in the rest room exemplified all the frustration and upset we sometimes experience when we continue to inappropriately attack life's problems, large or small.

People get frustrated and upset when they are working hard at something and still get no results. In the illustration above, it is obvious that people who continue to attack a problem over and over again in the same ineffective way are not as successful in resolving their problems as people who have learned to step back from the problem in order to get a different perspective on possible new solutions. When the woman was unable to get soap from the soap dispenser by pushing up on the handle, she needed to ask herself if she had labeled the problem correctly. For example, if the soap dispenser was empty, she was attacking the wrong problem. The problem, in that case, would be to find some soap. If she had labeled the problem correctly and there was soap in the soap dish, then the problem was how to get it out. Clearly, pushing up was not the answer. What other possibilities were there — pushing back, pushing down, unscrewing the bottle? Sometimes we approach a family problem or a work problem like this woman approached the soap dish. Perhaps we have had the same marital argument over and over again. We need to step back and ask ourselves, "How can I handle this problem differently since what I am doing is not working?"

Closing

The closing stage of the formula for handling upset people is very simple. At most it has three parts. First of all, ask the upset person if there is any other way we can be helpful. This is also the best time to educate the person about those things that will prevent future upset. For example, to the patient who neglected to bring their insurance information with them, the receptionist might say in closing, "By the way Mrs. Klein, if you remember to bring your insurance card at your next appointment, we can save you some time and some paperwork. Secondly, thank the person. We can thank them for any number of things: for letting us know of their dissatisfaction; for continuing to stay involved with us; for giving us new information. Finally, some kind of follow-up may be appropriate. Asking how things are going or calling to check on the status of the problem encourages the upset person to continue to be involved with us. One of the nicest stories about follow-up was reported by a workshop participant.

Bev had driven to a nearby town to return some sheet music. The sheet music was not what Bev expected it to be when she purchased it. Despite being annoyed at having to drive forty miles to exchange her purchase, Bev did feel that the owner of the store had been helpful. By the time she was leaving the store, an icy rain was falling and the weather grew threatening. That evening, safe and snug at home, Bev answered a phone call from the owner of the music store. The owner had been concerned because the weather had become so bad. She was calling to make sure her customer had arrived home safely.

Closing and follow-up can involve small but meaningful bits of symbolic communication. Examples include:

- writing our phone number down and handing it to a grieving friend with instructions that they are to call if they need something.

- asking our child whose teaching a new and difficult household chore to share his or her progress.

- leaving a special note for a loved one after an upsetting or angry interaction.

The closing stage of the process is similar to escorting our house guest to the door. It puts finishing touches on the interaction. It's the way we say, "The End."

Activity for Developing Closing Skills

Practicing in advance of a situation is one of the more helpful techniques for developing closing skills.

a) Think of a difficult closing situation such as:

- telephone conversations.

- getting someone out of your office or home.

- putting your children to bed.

- closing a meeting.

b) Select a situation to work on.

c) Anticipate what will happen.

- use memory of similar past events.

- use fantasy of expected events.

d) Practice lines to yourself, in mirror, to a friend. Rework the lines as often as necessary until you feel that you will be successful.

e) Practice in the real situation.

f) If it didn't go as you hoped, go back to "d."

We have covered the basic behaviors involved in dealing with upset people. Now let's look at some special cases of upset that require sensitive management. Chapter Eight describes techniques for dealing with angry people. Chapter Nine will discuss dealing with people who have experienced loss.

■

CHAPTER EIGHT
DEALING WITH ANGRY PEOPLE

EIGHT

It had been a long and frustrating day at the office. It seemed to Steve that not one thing had gone smoothly all day long. Suddenly, and catching Steve off-guard, the company controller appeared in the main work area of the department and began yelling at Steve. "How many times have I told you that unless I have your monthly report in my hands on time, I cannot get the projections done on schedule? I am sick and tired of waiting for your stuff. If something doesn't change fast around here you had better believe that I will do something to change this situation." Despite Steve's fatigue and frustration, he knew he had to keep his cool. After all, he was in full view of the entire office staff and was dealing with a man who had significant power in the organization.

This chapter is concerned with how to handle angry people. Angry people are upset people. Moreover, *we* become upset people when we find ourselves in the position of having to deal with an angry person. Before we describe a general formula and specific skills and strategies for handling anger, we'd like to discuss two important questions: "What is anger?" and "What causes it?" We are better equipped to cope with angry people if we understand the specific incident that triggered their upset and we may have some success in *preventing* another person from becoming angry if we understand the kinds of situations that are likely to be anger-provoking.

What Is Anger?

Anger is a feeling! Like other feelings, anger is part of the child in each of us as discussed in Chapter Three. Angry people sometimes act quite childlike, throwing tantrums, raising their voices, gesturing wildly. However, some angry people will go to great lengths *not* to appear childlike. They will camouflage themselves as critical parents, caring parents or rational adults. An angry person masquerading as a critical parent, for example, tells us what we *should* have done or *ought* to be doing. This kind of angry person symbolically points a finger at us and while shaking it in our face says such things as:

> "You should be home more. You spend more time working and socializing with your friends than you do at home with your family." (Translation: "I'm angry and hurt that you don't want to spend more time with me.")

Angry people sometimes pretend to be caring parents. These children in nurturing parent disguise are passively angry rather than attacking directly. It's not unusual for their tone to be sarcastic and for them to treat the objects of their anger as stupid children who lack the skills, knowledge or motivation to be helpful.

> "Dinner isn't ready because I was certain that you'd be too busy to call and tell me you'd be late. I certainly didn't want your dinner to be cold when you *finally* came home." (Translation:

"I'm angry that you are late getting home.")

Finally, angry people sometimes present themselves as quite cool and rational. Don't be fooled by super rational angry people. They too are wolves in sheep's clothing— angry people in their child ego state masquerading as adults. They may sound adult-like in their words Channel One, but the manner and body language channels often expose the angry child underneath.

> "Let me try and explain the importance of your getting home from work at a reasonable hour. The children are hungry. They need your attention. And there are household tasks to be done." (Translation: I am angry that you aren't home sooner.")

Emotions other than anger sometimes masquerade as anger. People who are worried, frightened or bereaved may appear to be angry. The anger helps to protect them from feelings of excessive vulnerability. It is important to recognize the vulnerability in the upset person's anger. If we respond to them as if they are only angry, we will have failed their greater need. We will say more about this later.

Responding to the Angry Child Ego State

We continually need to remind ourselves that angry people approach us out of their child ego state. Realizing this, we can make two important responses: *the caring response* and *the rational adult response*.

People frequently make two mistakes in dealing with anger. The first is to respond to the child in the angry person as a critical parent rather than a caring one. The second mistake is to move directly to adult, bypassing the caring parent altogether. Let's look at some possible responses from the person late getting home from work to the spouse who is angry.

> **Mistake #1** (Critical response. No caring; no rationality): "Why should I bother to hurry home? Dinner's never ready anyway."

> **Mistake #2** (Rational response. No caring): "When the boss asks me to stay late and work on a project, I don't have a choice if I want to get ahead. And we could use the money a raise would bring."

> **Appropriate Response** (Caring parent and adult): "I know you wish I could get home earlier. It's tough to be the first one home after work. What can I do to help now?"

As in complaint handling, it is necessary first to understand the person's anger and then work toward resolving the problem. More on this when we get to the formula.

The Roots of Anger

Anger is the result of many factors including the triggering situation, past experience and individual responses to experience. There are, however, certain situations that predictably lead to anger. As was mentioned in Chapter One, anger is sometimes the result of inappropriate handling of a minor complaint. In cases like these, people are not initially angry but become angry because of something we have either done or failed

to do. Obviously, this type of anger is preventable.
Positive contact skills and mastery of the upset formula
are invaluable. Other triggers for anger are more
complex. Understanding what creates anger in another
person is often helpful in planning both preventative
strategies and in deciding how to handle anger once it
occurs. In addition to secondary upset created by poor
complaint handling, there are seven other triggers for
anger that we will discuss. Let's look at each of these and
at strategies for preventing or managing them.

Dependency

To feel dependent is to feel we need something over
which we have no control. Whatever it is that we need,
we feel we are unable to provide it for ourselves and we
are dependent on someone or something else to meet that
need for us. Issues of dependency and control are closely
related. When we can't meet our own needs, we have
little control over how those needs get addressed. This
lack of control makes us angry or, at best, ambivalent.

Examples of the link between dependency and anger are
manifold.

- We need the services of public utilities. We feel
  utility companies control the costs. We feel
  dependent and often angry.

- Someone is providing our financial support. We
  feel dependent. We feel controlled and,
  therefore, angry. Or we may feel ambivalent.
  Even if we like being supported, we hate feeling
  dependent and controlled.

- We have damaged merchandise. The store

> controls the outcome of the complaint. We
> experience angry feelings anticipating that our
> need to return the merchandise may not be met.
>
> • We're in a hurry to have lunch. We've ordered
>   our meal and are waiting for our food. We feel
>   dependent on the cook and server to get us out
>   on time. We become irritated and, if we have to
>   wait too long, angry.

People experiencing feelings of dependency and anger
can, of course, manage their own feelings by reminding
themselves of the behavior that is in their control. They
often can discontinue doing business with those whose
goods or services are inadequate. They can choose to
work towards financial independence. They can switch
long distance phone service, turn down their air-
conditioners, insulate their homes, carry a sack lunch etc.
Any steps they take to feel more in control and less
dependent helps them to manage their own anger.

But how do we handle the angry dependent person who
is already out of control? When dealing with those who
are feeling angry as a result of dependency, we can do
those things that encourage them to recognize the extent
of their own control over the situation. For example, we
can give them limited choices. Utility companies do this
when they give customers a choice between regular
monthly billings or average monthly billings. Similarly,
some stores offer customers a choice of credit or new
merchandise when customers return damaged products.
Limited choices are available in personal situations, too.
An adolescent child may be given the choice of a monthly
allowance or a weekly allowance as a solution to money

matters. The child who is angry at bedtime can be given a choice about going directly to bed at 8:30 or getting into bed at 8:15 and reading to for fifteen minutes before bedtime. A spouse who expresses irritation about lack of attention can be asked what in particular would help him or her to feel appreciated. The important point here is that giving people choices is very useful in bypassing or reducing anger. The feeling of having no choices can provoke anger.

The other key to dealing with anger triggered by dependency is the obvious one—helping others to become more independent. Many situations are ripe for us to share information or teach skills. As parents, for example, all of us have a responsibility to teach our children those things that will promote their growth into independent adults. Obviously the child who can't tie his or her own shoelaces has more opportunity to feel angry towards a busy parent than one who has the skill to tie the laces and run out to play. The adolescent who earns his or her own spending money and therefore earns the right to spend part of it as he or she sees fit is less likely to feel angry at parents than the adolescent who has to ask permission for every purchase. The more we teach our children, the less dependent and the less angry they feel. The ultimate goal of parenting is to develop our children into self-sufficient adults.

Authority

Authority issues can trigger anger. Either too much or too little structure and direction can be problematic. Imagine for a moment giving a child a chore such as cleaning out the garage. The highly authoritarian person says, "This is what you will do. This is exactly when you will do it. This is exactly how you will do it." There can be no deviation. The possibility of having to deal with an angry, upset child out of this orientation is high. As in dependency issues, over directed people feel out of control and without any choices. In addition, highly authoritarian people often provoke anger in those they are directing as much because of their manner as because of their requests. People get more upset over "how" directions are given than they do over "what" directions are given. Most of us respond better to requests than to orders.

On the other hand, upset and angry reactions may also result from incomplete or unclear directions for performing a task. The less skilled the person is who will carry out the task, the more frustrated he or she will become if there are insufficient guidelines. New tasks, in particular, need to be well explained. The child who has never cleaned the garage needs both instruction and positive support until he or she has developed the necessary new skills.

Frustration and anger can be prevented by matching your authoritativeness and your directiveness to the situation. The capable, self-motivated person, carrying out a familiar task, probably thrives when left alone. The inexperienced person, executing an unfamiliar task or a brand new activity, needs more detailed instruction and closer supervision. The concept of matching the amount of direction you provide to the situation is useful in all supervisory situations. The new worker needs more direction than the employee who has been doing the job for a while. Likewise, small children and children mastering new situations require firmness and direction. Older children, adolescents and children familiar with a particular situation need a more democratic parenting style. In a recent consultation with a Girl Scout administrator, it became clear that several of her new volunteer troop leaders were floundering because of lack of direction. This administrator prided herself on her ability to leave her volunteers alone. We helped her to see that she needed to be more specific with these new volunteers who not only lacked the know-how to perform their function but lacked confidence as well. The important point to remember is to adjust your parenting style to match the needs of the child or your supervisory style to match the needs of the person whom you are supervising. In all situations, you are well advised to maintain Channel Two, manner, at an appropriate level and to vary Channel One, your verbal directiveness, to match the person with whom you are dealing.

Unclear Limits

Observe people in an unclear situation and before long you will see their frustration escalate into irritation and eventually anger. Our favorite example of this took place at a conference several years ago. The registration process had registrants searching confusedly for a registration line. When the line was finally discovered, a forty-five minute wait ensued. Believe it or not, when registrants reached the front of the line, they were given a registration form and told to fill it out and then go to another, equally long line. We think you can imagine the level of anger with which the conference planners had to cope.

Prevention is the key to handling anger created by unclear limits. In any situation, put yourself through the paces of those who will be in it — the new volunteer, the customer, the trainee, the participant, the student, the child, etc. Look to see what limits and boundaries are necessary. Specific instructions, clearly posted signs and well spelled-out rules are useful for clarifying limits. Telling children what is expected of them as well as what will happen if they don't meet expectations demonstrates setting clear limits and boundaries. Checking to be sure a patient knows where to check in, where to wait, how long he or she can expect to wait and perhaps even what will happen to him or her once in the doctor's examining room can do much to prevent anger and upset. Checking physical territory to outline limits and boundaries and helping others to define psychological limits and boundaries are necessary parts of the process.

> While traveling in Florida I (Pennie) had a serious bout of food poisoning. Having previously noticed a walk-in family emergency center, I hurried back to it in the hopes of getting some quick symptom relief. This clinic did a superb job of clarifying limits; an excellent stance for those dealing with sick people. Signs told you exactly where to go and what the payment policy was. The receptionist made a clear statement about how long I'd wait. The nurse

who took some blood and urine samples was precise in expectation setting, instructing and in letting me know it would take fifteen minutes to get the results. She asked if anyone was with me so that she could go out to the waiting room and let that person know I was being detained for lab work. The doctor gave me written instructions for diet and medication and asked me to call if I had further questions. This kind of clarity is excellent for reducing possible points of concern or bewilderment that so frequently lead to anger and upset.

Complexity

The more complex a situation is, the more opportunity there is for something to go wrong and, therefore, for people to get angry. When complexity is the cause of anger, simplification is the prevention or the cure. A case in point is the change by many banks and airlines from multiple waiting lines to a single feeder waiting line. Customers' exasperation mounted when they observed other lines moving more rapidly than the one in which they were waiting. This procedural simplification from multiple lines to one single line helped both customers and customer service personnel by cutting down on upset.

Similarly, simple requests, directives and rules help deter family conflict. Long complex explanations about why the children need to be in bed by eight o'clock are not necessary. Over-explaining, one aspect of complexity, creates more upset and anger than it reduces." It is bedtime" is the simplest directive to give a child.

Scanning the other person's channels and being responsive to what you observe is an excellent approach for preventing upset in potentially complex situations. If you see people wandering about with confused expressions, assume they are unclear about what to do or where to go. Asking "Can I help you?" may prevent a bewildered person from becoming an angry one. Sometimes you can see frustration mounting as you attempt to give complex instructions to someone. When this is the case, a switch in tactics is advised. Jot down instructions. Walk the person through the steps or take care of the process yourself. Any time a complex situation can be simplified or broken down into a series of less complicated steps, you enhance your chances of preventing unnecessary anger.

Prior Unresolved Conflict

Another cause of anger is prior unresolved conflict; anger about something that happened in the past which was not satisfactorily resolved. In marriages, for example, we may find ourselves bewildered by an angry spouse for whom some small incident triggered old feelings related to a difficult relationship with his or her parents. People may get angry at an insignificant slight because an old wound has never healed. Perhaps they are still stewing about a thoughtless remark we made at last year's Thanksgiving dinner.

> Helen complained that her daughter-in-law seemed edgy and angry whenever they were together. After noticing that family get-togethers were continually being affected by the daughter-in-law's sour disposition, Helen decided to have

a talk with her daughter-in-law about this problem. What surfaced from their conversation was the daughter-in-law's long-held angry feelings because Helen had objected to her son's marriage ten years earlier. This old anger toward her mother-in-law had never been resolved and was damaging the current relationship.

When anger is the result of prior unresolved conflict, then it is appropriate to surface the old conflict in an attempt finally to get resolution. Helen, in the example above, is beginning this process. It is obvious that Helen and her daughter-in-law will have to work out these old feelings from ten years ago if they are ever going to enjoy their relationship.

Communication Problems

Anger is sometimes the unpleasant result of a communication problem. What is actually sent and then actually received in a conversation can resemble "two ships passing in the night." When you suspect that a communication problem is the source of escalating anger, clarify the situation by using clarifying questions, paraphrasing and checking for understanding as outlined in Chapter Seven. Using the dual skills of asking clarifying questions and paraphrasing helps you focus on the content of the sender's message. Checking for understanding allows you to focus on what the sender is feeling.

"It sounds like this aspect of your job is taking much more of your time than you anticipated."

"You feel I am unfair in setting your school-night curfew at 10 o'clock and wish that it could be later."

If you suspect that the other person is having trouble getting your message, you can request a paraphrase or a check for understanding.

"I want to be sure you understand the issues I'm raising. I know we talked about a lot of different things. Share with me what you think I'm requesting with regard to how you approach the problem?"

Conflict of Interest

Finally, anger is often the result of a conflict of interest. Your spouse wants Chinese food for dinner; you want Mexican. The church youth choir wants their annual tour to travel west; the choir director prefers to go east. Different interests with mutually exclusive positive outcomes can become fertile soils for angry disputes.

Conflict Resolution Strategies

Situations involving a conflict of interest are challenging. There are many different ways to try to resolve conflicts of interest. Each strategy can be useful, but it also can be abused. Obviously, in handling conflict situations, the goal is to select the strategy that stands the best chance of successfully resolving the problem. A description of five conflict resolution strategies, along with a discussion of the benefits and costs of each strategy, follows.

Competing

The conflict resolution stance of *competing*, a stance where one party wins and one party loses (a win/lose situation) can result in the short-term winner becoming the long-term loser.

> A quilted raincoat was returned by the cleaners with the fabric looking like an over-washed mattress pad. It was clear that the cleaner had mistaken it for a washable garment and inappropriately laundered rather than dry cleaned it. The cleaner felt the customer should have specifically designated the coat to be dry-cleaned and refused to compensate the customer. The angry customer switched cleaners and has been a faithful customer of the new cleaners for thirty-eight years. For the last twelve or more years, the customer's grown children have also used their mother's recommended cleaners. Who won?

Win/lose strategies are not recommended when you are aiming for a long-term, healthy relationship. A competitive conflict resolution strategy, therefore, is best used when your aim is to have the other party change his or her behavior in the future or leave the relationship. If, for example, you decide that the only way you are willing to maintain your marriage is if your spouse stops drinking, then you may choose a confrontational, win/lose tactic. Only if you intend to leave your present job if a raise is not forthcoming should you consider an ultimatum to your boss.

Accommodating

In an *accommodating* conflict resolution stance, you choose to lose and let the other party win. In general, use accommodating when you sense that the outcome is very important to the other party and/or when you feel that your current losses will be outweighed by future gains. Agreeing to go on a ski vacation when you had dreams of sunning on the beach in Florida is an example of accommodating. Perhaps vacation plans are more important to your spouse than they are to you. Or, you may decide that a happy spouse who acts lovingly while on vacation is more important than warm weather. Accommodation can be relationship building. However, what usually does not work are relationships in which one person does all the accommodating. Eventually, that person is almost sure to tire of the role.

Compromising

Compromising is a third strategy for resolving a conflict of interest. In compromising nobody wins all and nobody loses all. It is a strategy based on the philosophy that half a loaf is better than none. Compromising is best used when the two parties have mutually exclusive goals. It often forces the opposed parties to ask for more than what they want, knowing they will have to settle for less. The sale and purchase of residential property is a good example of this. The goals of the two parties are mutually exclusive. The buyer wants top dollar; the seller wants to pay as little as possible. Both state a dollar figure more extreme than what they anticipate settling for. In fact, if a seller takes our first offer, we worry that we offered too much.

The cost in compromising is that neither party is totally satisfied. Sometimes both sides feel as if they have lost. If you end up skiing one winter and sunning the next, one of you may feel cheated during every vacation.

Interests may conflict, but not all conflicts of interest have mutually exclusive goals. More often than not, goals are similar for both parties. For example, the spouses who couldn't decide between a Chinese or a Mexican dinner may have had mutual goals in wanting to get away from the children for an evening and in not wanting to cook and clean up. Two youth group leaders may be in conflict about what activities to implement. But they will probably be in agreement in their desire to keep the kids involved and active.

Collaborating

When conflicting parties focus on their goals rather than on particular alternatives they can *collaborate*. Collaboration is a win/win strategy. The needs of both parties are met. It involves finding mutually acceptable solutions that help both parties to feel successful. The earlier illustration of the family who solved their vacation dilemma by combining driving and flying exemplifies the value of collaboration. One drawback to collaboration is that it can be time consuming because it often requires a lengthy problem-solving process. And collaboration may be difficult if disagreeing parties cannot agree on goals.

Avoiding

A final conflict resolution strategy is *avoiding*. Avoiding means ignoring the problem. Avoiding strategies are valuable when people need to pick the issues worth fighting over rather than fight over everything. Avoidance is a "peace at all costs" maneuver. It is best used as a strategy of choice when there will be little damage if the conflict is left unattended and where there is a greater positive than negative outcome from not solving the disagreement. Imagine, for example, that you have just reprimanded one of your employees. As he leaves your office, you hear him muttering some grumpy words under his breath. Avoidance may well be the strategy of choice. You want him to be sure to focus on the issue for which he was reprimanded. If at this point, you refocus his attention onto his attitude, you risk fighting over the wrong issue.

An avoiding stance can be problematic. Avoidance may leave one or both of the conflicting parties unsatisfied with the outcome. Hostility can build up over time and the eventual conflict may be more difficult to deal with than the avoided conflict. We often call this "the straw that broke the camel's back" syndrome. Avoiding may be a cop-out rather than a strategy if people choose to avoid because they are afraid of the other person's anger or have no skills for problem resolution. Avoiding should not be the inevitable outcome of not knowing what else to do.

All conflict resolution stances have some pluses and some minuses. Each of us needs a broad range of skills for settling conflicts of interests. Practice using all the strategies. Match your strategy to the situation.

The Formula For Handling Anger

Once we have some idea of what anger is and what causes it, we are ready to think about a process for defusing anger in other people. The formula for dealing with anger uses the same basic five ingredients as the formula for dealing with upset: listening, empathizing, clarifying, problem solving and closing. When confronted by an angry person, you use these ingredients in a formula that can be broken down in the steps listed below.

Listening

Listening involves all the skills and behaviors discussed in Chapter Seven — only more so. The higher the level of the upset, the harder it is to listen. In dealing with angry people, we really have to work at listening. Listen for the content, the feelings and those things with which you can agree. Listen with your caring, understanding parent state and your rational adult state. Listen without your critical parent state, without personalizing and without counterattacking. Cover your bases by getting information. Cover your hot buttons by not being drawn into an argument. And cover your rear by not putting yourself into positions you'll later regret.

Acknowledging Feelings

Acknowledge that the other person is angry. Do *not* try to talk him or her out of feeling angry. Simply understand what the person is experiencing.

Agreeing

State areas of agreement. This requires a totally different mindset from the one that most of us have learned to use in upset interactions. It means that we are not listening to catch the other person when they exaggerate, get confused or overreact. Rather, we are listening for those things with which we can agree.

> After a particularly difficult day of training, we decided to reward ourselves with a long, leisurely and expensive dinner in one of the better-known restaurants in the area. When a costly seafood dish arrived at the table boasting only two shrimp and two scallops, our anger immediately escalated. Don said "No, no way. There are only two small shrimp and two scallops in this dish. I am not going to accept this meal at the price you are asking." The waitress handled herself beautifully. Using the principle of stating areas of agreement she said, "I understand your upset, sir. I know you were expecting more seafood in your serving. Let me return your plate to the chef and see what we can do. Turning to Pennie, she asked, "May I take your meal to the kitchen and keep it warm so that you will both be able to enjoy your meal together?"

The above waitress just as easily could have focused on how poorly we were behaving, how we were the first people to complain or how expensive shrimp and scallops are. Instead she understood, agreed and was appropriately appreciated through a generous gratuity.

By the same token, if there is a family dispute over the equitable use of the family car, there can be agreement over the goal that everyone in the family needs some sort of transportation. When all else fails, we can always agree to disagree.

After you have listened, understood and stated areas of agreement, you may find that before you can move to a problem-solving mode you need more information. As was suggested in Chapter Seven, clarifying involves asking neutral, factual questions from your adult state to the angry person's adult state.

Getting Agreement on the Problem

When you are satisfied you have sufficient information, restate the problem in your own words.

> My (Don's) daughter came in an hour and a half late from a school activity. She came in looking like she'd been having a grand time and announced that the group decided to go for pizza after the school play. The response of an angry parent quickly deflated her mood. Finally she said: "I don't think 10:30 is an unreasonable hour." "Neither do I," I answered. "I'm upset because I didn't know where you were and I was worried. I am angry because you didn't call and tell me you'd be late. I expect you to call when you will be later than agreed upon."

In this case my daughter and I did not initially agree on the definition of the problem. I was angry because I was worried and upset that something might have happened to my daughter. My daughter was upset because she thought I was saying that she could not stay out till 10:30

or could not go out with her friends for pizza. It was important to get some agreement on the problem. We eventually agreed that the problem was one of someone being later than expected. Everyone must agree on what the problem is if there is to be a solution. Otherwise, we may argue about and solve the wrong thing. Sometimes defining the problem is the hardest part of the process.

Finding Solutions

A phone call to request a change in schedule was the agreed upon solution for future situations in the scene described above. But many possible solutions could have been listed before selecting a mutually acceptable one.

1) Call if you are going to be late.

2) A one-hour grace period.

3) Come home first and ask for permission.

4) No more curfews.

5) No exceptions — get home on time.

6) Check with friends before you leave and make sure you are clear about plans.

7) Grounded for a specified period of time whenever you are late.

8) Stop going out with friends.

For some simple problems we quickly compute the possible solutions, almost unconsciously and then select an appropriate one. For more complex problems, we may list the possible solutions internally, verbally or in writing. When dealing with angry people, it is often wise to problem solve together; agreeing first on the problem, identifying possible solutions and then agreeing on one solution. That solution is then implemented. In some situations, the selected solution can be evaluated at a predetermined time. If it is not working, another solution is selected and implemented. This problem-solving process was described in detail in Chapter Seven.

Closing

"Is there anything else I can do?" "Are you feeling satisfied at the outcome?" "If you have any further difficulty, please call." "Here's my card." "Let me jot down my name and number for you in case you need something else." These are all early closing remarks. If you truly believe that the sharing of upset, angry feelings provides useful feedback and indicates a wish to continue the relationship, you can put the icing on the cake by using your personal variation of the following statement:

> "Thank you for letting me know that you were angry (upset, dissatisfied, etc.). I certainly want to keep things straight between us. When I know what the problem is, we have a better chance of solving it."

Eight Hints for Handling Anger

Specific behaviors work well in handling angry people and can be useful when applied at various stages of the formula. The person who successfully deals with angry people has mastered the appropriate use of these eight behaviors. Several of these helpful hints have also been described elsewhere in the book.

1) *Communicate confidence and composure.* You need to be in control of yourself since angry people frequently are not in control of themselves. Your composure is reassuring to both of you.

2) *Ask for information.* Your goal, once you have addressed the child ego state of the angry person, is to move the angry person into the adult ego state. Once in a problem-solving mode, it is more difficult to stay angry.

3) *Use "I" messages.* If you must talk about the issues as they relate to either of you, use "I" messages. An "I" message is a statement that puts things in terms of how they effect you rather than the other person. "I" messages keep you from placing blame, whereas blaming fuels the fire of an angry person. *"I'm* sorry, but *I* am unable to allow your friends to drink beer in our home," is a more appropriate response to a teenager's request than, "You and your friends can't drink here and *you* are being irresponsible to even ask."

4) *Depersonalize angry interactions.* Remind yourself that sometimes angry, upset people are just unloading on you. They generally are not angry at you, but are angry at the situation.

5) *Aim for a mutual definition of the problem.* State the problem. Remember that symbolically, your goal is to place the problem on the table between you and

the angry person rather than assume the problem belongs personally to either one of you. "It seems we are having a hard time deciding on a reasonable time schedule for this project," is preferable to "You are making unreasonable demands." The problem is defined as one of deciding on the curfew, not someone's unreasonableness.

6) *Give people choices.* Angry people feel out of control. If they are given options, it helps them to see that they have some control. We admire the way one of our friends permits her children to experience choice around some of the tasks they hate to do. Many times we've smiled to ourselves as she's asked, "Do you want to set the table now or wait until the next commercial?"

7) *Hold firm assertively.* When you are doing all you can do, it is neither necessary to back down or to raise your own anger level. "I'm sorry that my traveling upsets you. My job requires occasional travel and I am going to be out of town a day or two a month." Long explanations, apologies, outrage or anger are not needed.

8) *Praise yourself.* Remember that dealing with angry people is hard work. You will not always handle everything skillfully. However, you are trying hard and working to be more effective. Take a moment to pat yourself on the back.

Ten Techniques for Handling the Very Angry Person

Most of us have faced someone whose overwhelming

anger violates the possibility for normal communication. While this book is not a crisis management primer, it is important to stress that there are limits to what any of us is expected to tolerate from angry, out of control people. We should not maintain communication with the profane, verbally obnoxious or abusive person. You are always free to draw the line when your sensibilities have reached their limits. Safety is absolutely a primary consideration in the face of physical danger; your safety, the safety of others and the safety of property. People safety is always more important than property.

Uncontrollable anger is rare. Anger is a normal feeling and is less likely to get out of control when it can be appropriately expressed. We'd like to share some specific strategies for you to use in order to help others maintain or regain control of their anger. Select the strategy or strategies based on each situation. Again, practice is the key.

1) *Soft to hard.* This technique is synonymous with the last of the six principles for handling upset people discussed in Chapter One. Respond to angry people at the lowest confrontational level possible. This may mean anything from repeating a person's name three or four times to calling the police or security guard. The point is to match the intervention to the level of anger—not to use a heavier hand than is necessary.

2) *Personalize.* Using a person's name is another technique for dealing with angry people. It is easier to behave badly when you think you are anonymous.

Some people prefer to get angry over the phone rather than face-to-face in order to remain anonymous. Names remind angry people that you know who they are. Names are also safe words to use. If someone is yelling at you, you can always say his or her name several quick times in succession to interrupt, "Ginny, GINNY, GINNY." When we don't know the person's name, we can use Sir, Ma'am or Miss; "Sir, SIR, SIR."

Personalizing can also be used to help the angry person remember just what it is that is angering him or her. You can ask, "Is there anything about my behavior that is upsetting you?

3) *Off feet and away from others.* No one needs an audience when interacting with an angry person. Spectators cause all of us to feel that we need to win in order to save face. Your first goal is to get the angry person away from others and then, if possible, off his or her feet. It is more difficult to yell when you are sitting down.

> An agitated client entered the waiting room of our office and began demanding to see a particular counselor, Dr. S. She was talking loudly and standing over the receptionist in a menacing fashion. Her behavior was upsetting to those in the waiting area as well as to the receptionist. Noticing an empty office a few feet away, the receptionist asked the client to follow her. She grabbed a pad and pencil from her desk on the way. As they walked toward the office the receptionist said, "I'll have you wait for Dr. S. in here. Let me get your name so that I can let

her know you need to see her."

4) *Yes . . . . and.* Yes . . . but is a response many of us
   are familiar with. When we hear, "yes. . . but" we are
   prepared to hear a qualified and watered down
   "yes."

   John: "I'm angry that you gave the new project
   to Marvin. I would like the opportunity
   for some of the more challenging jobs.."

   Jane: "I understand, but Marv has been here
   longer than you and his work has been
   excellent. Maybe next time."

We propose switching to yes . . . *and. And,* rather than
but, doesn't qualify your agreement. It maintains the
agreement full strength while clarifying it.

   Jane: "O.K., in the future I'll try to spread the
   challenging work around."

5) *Match and move.* Sometimes it is a mistake to
   maintain our cool while other people are blowing off
   steam. Our calmness seems or looks phony to them
   and only serves to infuriate them further. When this
   appears to be the case, we suggest a strategy called
   "match and move." If the other person is yelling,
   raise your voice to match them and then quickly
   move down the scale by lowering your voice.

   Harriet's sixteen year-old son was beside himself
   over having to mow the yard before he could go
   to the football game. He worked himself into a
   screaming fit. When Harriet tried to reason with
   him, he couldn't hear her over his own rage.
   Finally Harriet screamed "Shut up, sit down and
   listen." Once she had his attention, she quickly

lowered her volume and changed her tone as she
briefly restated the rule and her expectations.

6) *What else?* Our spouse, red-faced and breathing
hard, is barraging us with a barrel full of anger. His
or her angry shots are at everything from the way we
handle the children to the way we spend money, to
how we look, to our behavior at parties. Once you
have acknowledged that he or she is very upset, ask
him or her to be specific about gripes. Continue to
ask if there is anything else that is problematic until
he or she is out of complaints and out of steam.
Engaging the rational adult state helps other people
to gain control of their feelings. Asking others to list
all their complaints is also a statement of our willingness to work things out. And frequently the real
complaint does not surface first. It is the third or
fourth item on the list. If we don't bother to ask
"what else," we sometimes end up arguing over or
problem solving about the wrong thing. In the
process of asking a very angry person to list all his or
her gripes, the angry person will discover that the list
is finite, perhaps much less extensive than was
originally thought or felt. We can't stress enough the
importance of this tactic and how different it is from
defensively arguing with each point. Using the
strategy of "what else" requires lots of practice and
the lowering of personal defenses.

7) *Beating to the punch.* My (Pennie's) son was a master
of this anger-defusing technique. When he would do
something that infuriated me, he would wisely
approach me with, "Mom, you're gonna kill me. I'd

be mad, too, if I were you." It's very difficult to maintain an angry aggressive stance with a person who's admitting fault. When you're at fault and you both know it, try the "beat to the punch" approach. A similar stance has you simply agree with the upset person. "I'd be upset too if . . . " You can always agree with a person's wish. "I know you wish that this had not happened."

8) *Do what they're already doing.* When you feel that you will not be able to change how the angry person is behaving, tell him or her to do what he or she is already doing. "Go ahead and scream." "Let me get you a tissue." "Stand right here while I find the manager." "You can continue to pound the desk, if it helps."

9) *Ignore/Deny.* People who continue to make unreasonable demands forfeit the right to be taken seriously. In such cases you have the right to ignore their demands or to deny them. There is a time to say "I'm sorry, I do not believe you." We also may choose to ignore an occasional off-color word that slips into the speech of the upset person.

10) *Same song—Different verse.* People who continue to make demands or carry on unnecessarily should be told repeatedly that their demands will not be met or that they will not get their way by continuing to persist. Continue saying "No" in as many ways as you choose until your point is understood. Do *not* reward the other person's persistence by giving in. Children who get rewarded by persisting until they

get their way continue to be persistent, manipulative and hard to live with.

We have shared a number of strategies for coping with angry, upset people. We believe that only a small percentage of those with whom you interact will escalate to that very angry stage. More commonly, people who are handled positively rarely become upset or, if they have complaints, those complaints can be handled before anger erupts. For that small percentage of really angry people, however, you can achieve success by practicing all of the strategies outlined in this chapter. Mentally rehearse in your head. Think through how you will respond if faced with various problematic situations. Play out different approaches in front of a mirror or with a friend or family member. Finally, use these strategies in real life situations. Practice is important!

■

CHAPTER NINE
DEALING WITH LOSS AND GRIEF

NINE

Most of Harry's friends knew that he had made a hurried trip to the Mayo Clinic the previous week. Harry had been experiencing symptoms that were frighteningly similar to those associated with colon cancer. Now, as Harry's friends mingled and chatted at the church social, they were uncomfortably aware of Harry's wife Martha who looked depressed and fearful. When she was asked about Harry's condition, Martha dabbed at her eyes while explaining that Harry had definitely been diagnosed as having cancer. The doctors felt that because the cancer was so far along, Harry would probably not live long. No one at the social knew what to say to Martha.

In this chapter, we will be discussing how to deal with people who are grieving. Grief is the natural response to loss and change. The discomfort that Harry and Martha's friends felt in finding themselves face to face with Martha was typical and to be expected. Most of us are unsure about how to behave when we are faced with people who are struggling to cope with loss or change. To suffer a loss is to suffer a deprivation. Loss is a broad term that includes many things, from a lost promotion to a lost sporting competition, to the death of one's most intimate life companion. Grief embraces the full range of feelings that are generated by loss and change. The following list includes examples of the kinds of losses that can be expected to lead to upset.

Death:	The loss of a loved one, friend, pet, etc.
Depression:	The loss of hope.
Divorce:	The loss of a spouse, a relationship, a shared history, a lifestyle.
Illness:	The loss of health.
Retirement:	The loss of the focus of one's productivity.
Moving:	The loss of a home, roots, friends, neighborhood
Aging:	The loss of health, physical appearance, strength, some competencies, etc.
Possessions:	The loss of money, property, possessions, tangible material things

Dealing with people who are experiencing the pain of a loss can be very stressful. Not only do we not know how to act or what to say, but we are afraid that we will say or do the wrong thing and make the other person's upset even greater. We erroneously think we should be able to make the upset person feel better when, in fact, our primary task is to provide comfort.

In addition to our feelings of inadequacy, we may also experience feelings of vulnerability when faced with the upset person who is grieving.

After the death of a five year-old child to leukemia, members of the community not only grieved over the loss, but also identified with the pain in the death of a child, secretly harbored fears for their own children's health and safety and experienced feelings of relief that this tragedy belonged to someone else.

Such a boiling cauldron of feelings obviously has an impact upon our ability to handle grief and upset.

Before discussing the appropriate behaviors for dealing with people who are upset over loss, it is first necessary to understand what is happening to them. Losing something, as we all know, is painful. Losing something hurts. Losing something creates a variety of feelings — feelings of varying hues, shades and intensities. Yet, despite the range of feelings, people who are grieving experience a predictable sequence of emotions and behaviors.

A number of people have written about this predictable grieving process, most notably Elizabeth Kubler-Ross. Kubler-Ross identifies five stages to the grief process. We have incorporated Kubler-Ross' and other theories and techniques into our counseling practice. Through the years, we have developed our own specific ideas about grief work as we have counseled with those who are trying to cope with difficult and painful life changes. We have applied grief counseling to a broad range of "loss" or "change" problems such as divorce, empty nest syndrome, illness, aging, etc. We'd like to share with you our specific ideas for successfully dealing with upset people who are grieving over loss or change.

The Response Cycle To Loss

There are at least six predictable responses to grief. Once we can identify where the upset person is in the response cycle, we can tailor our own behavior to best help him or her.

> A vivid childhood memory illustrates the first phase in the response to loss cycle. I (Pennie) was only four years old the day my mother bundled me up and raced with me over to my aunt's house. My aunt had just received a telegram stating that her nineteen year-old son, her only child, was missing in action in WW II. What bewildered the child in me was my aunt's behavior. I knew "her little boy" might be dead and yet she was playing the role of the impeccable hostess — welcoming the family and guests, rushing around the kitchen preparing food — in fact behaving quite normally. The only clue that gave away her numbness to the telegram was a large cut on her leg; the result of banging into the corner of a cabinet. The cut was bleeding profusely, yet obviously unfelt by her. When I asked my mother about this she said, "Aunt Claire can't feel her cut just like she can't feel her sadness.

Aunt Claire's reaction (or perhaps we should say her lack of reaction) typifies the initial response to any painful loss: *shock and denial.* A large part of us is screaming, "Say it isn't so, this is not happening to me." The length of time a person in a grieving state denies his or her loss varies. In extreme cases people have been known to "pretend" forever that some particular life event never happened. More typically, the denial phase lasts just long enough for upset people to gather their strength in order to be able to cope with their loss. Denial is an early coping mechanism that helps people deal with their loss. In our contacts with those in mourning, it is useful to remember that denial is an important early coping mechanism for handling grief.

Denial

People in the denial phase of the grief cycle are not ready to accept their loss. In this phase, listening is especially important. Don't try to convince people of the reality of their loss. Do, however, quietly and calmly reiterate their situation. For example, to the grief-struck widow who is saying, "He just can't be gone. I can't believe he's dead," we don't say, "Harriet, you know Wesley is dead. You must accept this and come to terms with it." It is more helpful to say, "I understand how much you wish that Wesley was still alive. I know that you can hardly believe he's gone."

Only in cases where the grieving person continues to deny reality beyond a reasonable length of time might we consider some strategies for helping him or her to progress beyond denial. A reasonable length of time is, of course, often a matter of judgment. If we sense that denial is becoming either a lack of desire to face reality or a significant distortion of reality, this may indicate the upset person has exceeded normal limits for the denial phase. In such cases, gentle prodding, continuing reminders and statements of concern are invaluable. "Harriet, Wes has been dead for several months now. I'm worried that you seem unable to accept this." Or,

"Harriet, it concerns me that you are still acting as if Wes were alive. What would help you to come to terms with his death?" When denial becomes losing of touch with reality, referral for professional help is recommended.

Anger

A second response to loss/grief/change is *anger*. People want to blame someone or something for the bad things that happen. When a loved one dies, anger may be directed at God, at doctors, at the hospital. When a job is lost, anger may be focused on the company, at the government. When a child fails in school, anger may be directed at the child's friends, teachers, the school system. When a close friend moves away, we may be angry at the friend for leaving us. Examples of typical remarks from people in the anger phase of grief include: "It's not fair!" "The doctors don't know what they are doing." "It's all his (or her) fault." "You have no right to expect this of me."

The anger in grief is necessary and expectable. People who are hurting can express their pain by being angry. We have a responsibility to deal with their hurt rather than their anger. Most of us can see beneath the anger to the hurt and anguish of the person grieving over a death. For example, we know intuitively that the man whose wife was just killed in an accident is screaming with rage because of the pain of his loss. There are other times, however, when this may be less clear. Let's imagine that a close friend has just been fired. After leaving the job in disbelief, he or she begins telling us how unfair and what a horrible person the boss is. All of this may be expressed quite angrily. If we are not careful, we can easily fall into the trap of reacting to the anger rather than to the loss.

Anger is a necessary and expectable part of the grief process. The angry person, of course, also needs a good listener. Be careful not to argue with the anger. Sometimes, well-intentioned friends and comforters struggle with their own religious or moral values when confronted by a person who is expressing anger over his or her loss. We may feel it isn't "right" for a person to be angry at God, at someone who is dead or at the doctor. We need to stifle any reflexes we have that convey to the upset person that he or she shouldn't be angry. Rather, we need to give permission for the anger. "I can understand your anger." "I'd be angry too if I were left alone with three young children to care for." "Your rage at God is understandable." "You must feel so angry about how Katherine has suffered."

It is useful to allow the angry person his or her anger. We can't make other people's anger disappear. And, paradoxically, granting people permission to be angry often results in their letting go of the feeling. They feel understood!

Angry feelings that persist too long can impede the healing process and keep people from getting on with life. If we find the upset person maintaining an unhealthy anger for too long, referral to a professional may be in order. It may also be a time to be more confrontive.

Vera resisted her divorce with all her strength. Her husband, Charles, was determined to get out of the marriage. Once divorce was inevitable, Vera's anger smoldered and eventually raged. At first her friends thought it was good for her to rant and rave about Charles. Six months later, they were getting tired of hearing the same angry war stories over and over again. Vera began demanding that none of her friends talk to Charles or see him socially. Anyone who invited Charles to dinner became her enemy. Finally, her closest friend said, "Vera, I think you need to come to terms with this anger at Charles. I'm getting weary of listening to you and I suspect others are, too. I know you don't want to drive your friends away. And I know you don't want to live this way forever, harboring such hateful feelings. If you can't do it alone, how about making an appointment with your minister or a counselor and trying to work out your feelings about the divorce?"

Accommodating

Once people begin to adjust to their loss, self-talk (as described in Chapter Four) changes from "this can't be happening" toward a more rational self-talk aimed at reducing the negative feelings. During this phase, called the *bargaining* or *accommodating* phase, the upset person may begin to express regret, may try to make sense of the situation and/or may express a wish to have behaved differently in the past. Again, this is to be expected. "If only we had not had that argument." "If only I had gone to the hospital the night she died." "If God would only give me a chance to try again to be a better friend." "Well at least I won't experience more serious complications from this disease." "Thank God I only have diabetes instead of cancer."

These are the kinds of statements that can be expected from the person in the bargaining or accommodating phase. As you can see, upset people are looking for something positive in their loss. A congregation grieving over the upcoming departure of a beloved minister may refocus its grief onto some of the minister's qualities it won't miss. "Well, at least we won't have to put up with his messy study after he's gone" or "Let's hope our next minister has a better speaking voice." The divorcing wife may say, "I'll be glad not to have to listen to his snoring every night." It is healthy for bereaved people to look for the good in the bad. This is a sign that they are beginning to adjust to the loss. Bargaining and rationalizing help the upset person to adjust.

During the accommodating phase of the grief cycle, as upset people express regret and try to make sense of their situation, we can help them in several ways. As always, of course, we can listen and understand. "I know that you wish you had gone to the hospital the night Alice was so sick." "I know you wish you hadn't been unfaithful." "Retirement must be so difficult after so many years of an active work life." Statements of this type are appropriate. In addition, it is helpful to reassure the upset person. Reassurances need to fit the reality of the situation. They need to be "on target." "You did the best you were able to do at the time." "I would guess your wife would have understood that you needed to get some sleep that night." "You must have tried very hard to be a good employee."

Clarifying questions also serve a useful function for the upset person as he or she attempts to make sense of the loss. "Anything else you wish you would have said or done?" "What do you wish you had done differently?" "What are some of your memories of Alice?" "Do you feel like you've learned something in this process?" "If your mother was here now, what do you think she'd say to you?"

All of these clarifying questions not only help the bereft person to understand his or her own situation, but they also give the person an opportunity to share feelings and ideas.

Depression

At some point *mourning* and *depression* are inevitable. The sense of loss brings sadness, a loss of energy and a painful reflection on those things that will be missed. Bereft people often express that they are "just going through the motions." They may express feeling weary and exhausted. "I just don't have any energy." "I feel helpless." "I am so lonely." "I miss being healthy."

Mourning and depression are necessary if people are going to survive loss. It is natural to feel sad when you have lost something. All religions, in their wisdom, allow for a formalized grieving process, recognizing its value in healing the wounds of loss. Depression and mourning are coping skills for dealing with loss. It would be a statement of our lack of humanness if we were not saddened by loss.

It is difficult for many of us to deal with the upset person who is depressed. We don't like to see people unhappy. We have to fight our natural tendency to want to make the other person feel better. The grieving person does not feel better by being told to "cheer up." He or she will feel better only as the wounds heal. The guidelines for handling depression in others are brief. Be there for the depressed person! Listen! Understand! Don't say much! Comfort, support and permission to feel sad are what the grieving person needs.

Acceptance

Most of us are more comfortable dealing with people in the final two stages of loss acceptance and revitalization. Life goes on and people begin to refocus on the present and the future and to revise their expectations to fit the reality of the situation. People who have begun to accept their situation express some hopefulness about the future. In this phase, we often hear people saying things like: "Well, I guess I'd better get on with my life." "I don't like what happened but I guess I'll have to live with it." "My diabetes is a nuisance, but it's not as bad as some illnesses."

As upset people begin to *accept* their sorrow or loss, *our* task is to shift gears with them. We need to be able to join them in their recovery process. Our primary goal in dealing with people who are in the acceptance phase is to encourage their acceptance. We can accomplish this through our appropriate behavior on Channels One, Two and Three and by staying out of their way. We may need help with our own feelings of loss as those we comfort move on.

> Maria had been very close to her mother who had died six months earlier. Her own grieving process had been put on hold because her father had needed her support for his own overwhelming feelings of loss. After several months, her father met an attractive widow. Soon he was dating this woman and taking an active interest in life again. As her father accepted his loss and began to move on to revitalize, Maria was the one having difficulty coping with the death of her mother. It was hard for her to understand her father's recovery. Maria had not completed her own grieving. She resented his new companion not only for replacing her dead mother but also for replacing her as the primary caretaker of her father. Maria missed her mother and she also missed caring for her father.

Maria's father moved on and began planning a life after the death of his wife. It would be important for Maria not to share her own grief with her father if he was to continue to heal. But Maria now is faced with her own sense of loss. She could, of course, benefit from the patient and kindly ear of her family, a friend, a minister or a counselor.

Revitalization

Acceptance of a loss sometimes blossoms into a complete *revitalization*. Two years after Mary's husband left her, she had lost forty pounds, completed her college degree, embarked on a career with a pharmaceutical firm and become the director of her church's choir. Mary developed a whole new sense of herself once she worked her way through the loss cycle. She was surging with a vitality and energy she hadn't experienced in years. Jim's wife had suffered with an illness for several years. Jim had been intimately involved in her care. He had much adjusting to do after her death. The bulk of his time and energy had been consumed by his wife's needs. Once the grieving process had been accomplished, Jim was surprised by his new-found energy and his sudden focus on planning for the future. All the energy that had gone into the care of his wife could now be redirected into new activities. Jim learned to play bridge, joined a health club and became active in his church's singles' group. Once he accepted his wife's death, he was able to get on with his life.

In the revitalization phase, the previously upset person may develop new friends, new activities, new interests, a new mate. Acceptance and revitalization require our encouragement of the other person's development. As the grieving person resolves his or her painful feelings, we may, like Maria in the above illustration, be just beginning to experience our own feelings of loss. As situations change, friends may change. Retirees may no longer have much in common with old work friends. Widowed and divorced people may give up married friends and seek new single acquaintances. It is important to remember that we are not being rejected if this happens. Rather, it is a sign of the resolution of grief for the other person.

All of the six responses to loss are normal and necessary.

There is no exact length of time that is appropriate for each of the phases. Sometimes they don't follow in order. Sometimes they overlap. Sometimes a response will reappear when least expected. We can "be" with those who are grieving by accepting them in whatever stage of the grieving process they are in.

> The Youngs had given birth to a severely retarded child in 1974. Following their doctor's advice, which was based on the severity of the child's handicap, the Youngs placed their daughter in an institutional setting. Their grief had been overwhelming. Eventually, however, they accepted their loss and out of it developed a great satisfaction from their volunteer work with the local Retarded Children's Association. Despite their long-term acceptance, the Youngs continue to relive old emotions from time to time. Occasionally, anger and depression return to haunt them briefly. The appreciate their friends for accepting the painful times and for being there for them.

Three Factors that Affect the Experience of Loss

Denial, anger, accommodation, mourning, acceptance and revitalization each serve a function in helping people cope with loss or an unwanted change. Despite this predictable response cycle to grief, each person handles grief in his or her own individual way. The grief cycle varies in intensity and duration for each person. Some people cope with their sadness by crying; others by silence; others by talking; still others by listening to music.

When we are dealing with people upset over a loss, it behooves us to make a rough assessment about their ability to cope with their situation. Just as people differ in how they express grief, so, too, they differ in the variety and strength of their *coping mechanisms*. Obviously the greater the number and the strength of these coping mechanisms, the more quickly the upset person is likely to recover from a loss experience. For example, the person with sound judgment, good problem-solving skills and quick reflexes will be better able to restructure life if a fire destroys his or her home than will a person without these skills. Similarly the optimistic individual, who talks positively and rationally to himself or herself, has better odds of bouncing back after a loved one's death than the perennial pessimist.

In addition to assessing the upset person's coping skills, we need to answer two questions if we are to be as helpful as possible. The first question is: "What is the upset person's *perception* of his or her problem?" To illustrate the importance of perception, let's look at how two women, Jean and Chris, each viewed her own situation after a divorce. Neither woman wanted a divorce. Jean believed that if you weren't part of a couple, you had no real place in the world. Her previous identity as Mrs. James Fargo had been the source of her self-esteem. Without a husband, she felt she had little or no value. Chris, on the other hand, believed that while spouses' lives are intertwined, each person is an individual in his or her own right. She had a strong sense of who she was and did not believe that without a husband she was "nothing." She could not imagine her friends rejecting her because she had gotten a divorce. These differing perceptions about being single would greatly influence how each woman reacted to an unwanted divorce. Once we understand the perceptions each woman brings to her situation, we can have a clearer sense of how to best behave with each of them. Jean would probably need reassurance that she is acceptable and accepted. It would be very important to include her in couples' events, church gatherings and so forth. She might also profit from some help in developing new interests that would enhance her sense of competency and self-worth. Chris, on the other hand, might enjoy the opportunity to expand her already well-developed sense of herself as complete without a husband. A long, leisurely, chatty dinner with one or two close friends in addition to inclusion in church and social gatherings might be just what the doctor ordered. Chris might already be planning to join the church's singles' group, whereas Jean needs to be reassured that she still has her place with her coupled friends. Jean might need someone to offer her a ride to church; Chris might be offended if she feels her friends see her as unable to care for herself. The task is to match our responses to the upset person's perception of the dilemma while helping him or her to develop new perceptions as necessary. Ridicule in the form of, "Don't be silly. You're certainly old enough to take care of yourself, " or moralizing with statements such as, "You really should be mature enough to go to church alone," are never helpful. The best way to help people develop new perceptions and new skills is through support and encouragement.

The final question to ask ourselves as we approach an upset grieving person relates to *support systems.* Who or what can this person turn to for comfort and help? Does the upset person have friends, belong to clubs, have a church group, get along with the minister, have family, enjoy his or her job? The more comfort and support one has during painful times, the better. How we respond to an upset grief-stricken person would depend, in part, on what we know about his or her support system. Picture the busy minister who has just learned that two of his congregants have suffered a traumatic loss. This minister might appropriately choose to allocate more time to the friendless, retired widow whose only child lives out of town than to the married, busy mother of three children who has the support of many people in the community. In such a case, it would be clear who had the most need for support. Not only might the widow profit from attention, but the busy mother might need some time to be alone with her grief.

Loss And Transactional Analysis

Transactional analysis was first discussed in Chapter Three. Throughout the book, we have used ideas from T.A. as a framework for understanding and dealing with upset people. T.A. concepts can be applied to dealing with loss and change in two ways. First of all, the same basic T.A. rules exist for dealing with people experiencing a loss as for dealing with complaining or angry people. People who are grief-stricken are behaving out of their child ego state. The child, as you recall, is the repository of all feelings. Grief is a feeling state. The ego states that most apply to our handling of bereavement is the caring parent. Those who have incurred a loss need comfort, which resides in the domain of the caring parent. In addition, our rational adult state may be needed occasionally to help upset people respond to problems that result from loss. But only after we have first provided comfort. Also, the child within us can be helpful to the upset bereaved person. It is quite appropriate to cry with a dear friend whose child has just died or to be sad with an elderly person who is expressing pain about watching friends die. Sharing poignant feelings together can be comforting. As has been reiterated throughout the book, there is no place for the critical parent in dealing with upset.

There is a second way in which T.A. can be a useful tool as we learn to cope with those who are saddened. Until now, we have talked as if all losses are similar and, indeed, in many ways they are. There are, however, some ways in which losses differ from one another. These differences are more often in nature than in intensity. T.A. principles help us understand how losses differ from one another and how we might respond to different kinds of loss. Some losses are reality based. The loss of a loved one, being fired, losing your farm or business in a bankruptcy are all real losses. Conceptually, we might classify these real losses as belonging to the "adult."

> Margaret sought psychiatric help after the death of her daughter because she felt she was not recovering properly. When she told the psychiatrist that she was severely depressed over this death, he responded: "This is a different kind of case for me. Losing your child is so real. Most other people I see are depressed and have no real reason for it."

Other losses belong to the "child." "Child" losses are less tangible. Nothing "real" has vanished and yet people still feel bereft, sad and grief-stricken. The death of a wish, a dream, a hope or a goal is such a loss. Often as we talk to men and women who are getting close to retirement, they express feelings of loss either because they have not reached life goals that they had established for themselves or because all of their goals have been realized and they are feeling as if they have nothing left to which to look forward.

> A school music teacher augmented his income by giving violin lessons to beginning students. We learned in talking to him that he had graduated from the Julliard School of Music. His talent had been praised and he had expected an international concert career. His life didn't turn out that way. After a number of unsuccessful attempts to break into professional music, he returned to the Midwest. Still unable to make it in the local musical community, he took a job as an instrumental music teacher. Teaching eight-year-old beginning students, many of whom had little or no musical talent, was light years away from Carnegie Hall. This man was feeling lost and depressed — his hopes and dreams dashed.

While the loss of a dream is not as tangible as the loss of a loved one or the loss of a job, it can be, every bit as painful. It is important to be respectful of the mournful and depressed feelings of those who are saddened by the loss of wishes, dreams and hopes.

People can also experience "parent" losses. A loss of faith, a loss of belief and a loss of values are examples of "parent" losses. For example, growing up involves some loss for all of us. It is often depressing when we first learn that our minister, a beloved teacher, or our parents have human weaknesses. Many parent-child conflicts involve the parents' difficulty in adjusting to a loss. We usually call this kind of loss "coping with a changing world." Our grandparents or parents may have walked to school, but today's teenagers rely on their "wheels." The open discussion of sex and sexuality may have been taboo fifty years ago, but such is no longer the case. Parents may mourn the loss of a simpler (or a different) lifestyle. They may wish that things would be more like they used to be.

> Karen had allowed herself to have an extramarital affair with a man who had been a close friend for many years. She had held strong convictions about marital fidelity and was overwhelmed with feelings of guilt and shame. Her personal loss of a long-held value was painful to her. In addition to breaking off the affair, Karen had to grieve the temporary loss of an important value, of a belief in and about herself.

All three kinds of loss require comforting, caring, nurturing, listening and being there. In addition, reality based losses usually forecast significant life changes to which people will need to adjust. These might include: "How am I going to spend my time now that my children are grown and out of the nest?" "How can I learn to handle my finances without Tony?" "How can I make a living now that I have lost my job?"

Child state losses of hopes and dreams are best served by

quiet comforting. Since the loss of hopes, dreams and wishes doesn't require an immediate adjustment in current life situation, a good ear and lots of understanding will usually do the trick. We can also use our personal knowledge of the grieving individual to redirect goals, hopes and dreams.

> A corporate executive who came for counseling was feeling depressed as he approached retirement. Most of his career goals had been met. He felt he had nothing left in his future. During one of the counseling sessions, he described his life-long interest in history and how he had read widely about the Civil War. He had been thinking about some important ideas and had, at one time, even considered writing about them. With a little encouragement, he slowly began changing his feelings about retirement. Freedom from regular work and from the pursuit of career goals would permit him valuable time in which he could put his ideas on paper.

Encouragement is not the same thing as pushing and prodding. Encouragement means creating an atmosphere through listening and understanding that gives the grieving person the freedom to explore new possibilities.

Parent state losses of faith, belief or values also respond well to good listening skills. People struggling with loss of faith or belief are usually very hard on themselves. It is wise not to add to their burden by moralizing to them.

Applying the Seven Channels

Although I (Pennie) was only thirteen years old when my father died, I remember vividly my different responses to the various well wishers who visited the house after the funeral. Some visitors talked incessantly, probably out of their own awkwardness. A few tried to talk me out of my grief by saying such things as: "You should be glad he didn't suffer." "You should be pleased God wanted to call him home." "Your father wouldn't want you to be sad." Some permitted me to express my grief by reminiscing with me about my father, through their quiet acceptance of my grief, or by hugging me and letting me cry. This experience taught me, at an early age, what works best for the bereaved person — silence, understanding and permission to express one's pain.

To reemphasize, listening and empathizing are the heart and soul of what we have to say about dealing with those who are upset because of loss. It is important, to augment these central themes by discussing specific behaviors to which grieving people respond well. Let's begin by looking at how we might use each of the seven channels of communication to handle upset generated by grief, loss or unwanted change.

Language

Each of the channels of communication has the potential to help or hinder the grieving process. Strange as it may sound, the most helpful message to send to the grieving person on *Channel One*, the language channel, is no message at all. Silence is truly golden to the distressed, bereaved person. Quietly sharing the pain, the tears or the sadness is poignant and comforting to those experiencing sorrow. There is no need to think of the "right" thing to say in a house of mourning. All you have to do is let the bereaved person know you are there and that you care. Your presence and your attention send this message loud and clear. Since upset people may need to express their feelings, good listening skills are far more important than having a "way with words."

Manner and Body Language

Channel Two, the manner channel and *Channel Three*, body language, help to carry the message of caring to the upset person. Physical closeness and touching can be powerful healers. A hug, a pat on the shoulder, a lingering handshake or a caring look all convey the important message of "I'm here and I care" to the suffering person. Match the level of your behavior on Channels Two and Three to fit the person's loss, the intimacy of your relationship and the cues that you receive from the bereaved. Approaching a business acquaintance who has just lost her job will involve a simple handshake and "I'm sorry about the job." On the other hand, when an intimate friend experiences a significant loss, you will no doubt be on his or her doorstep within minutes and will use more intimate nonverbal behaviors to announce that it is all right to let down. The relief for the upset person can be enormous!

Territory

Channel Four, territory, involves some special application when dealing with loss and the upset that surrounds it. When people are complaining or angry, the last thing we want to do is violate their personal or psychological territory. But at times of bereavement, people often want and need intimacy. It is precisely at times of loss and grief that our social norms permit and even encourage the letting down of barriers that sometimes hinder closeness. Holding a grieving friend can provide much needed solace. Even a gentle touch on the shoulder or arm can imply a tender caring. Once again, it is important to match the intimate use of territory to the occasion and to the relationship. While hugging a close friend who is experiencing profound loss may be comforting, hugging the casual acquaintance who has recently retired may only add to his or her discomfort.

Psychologically as well as physically, grieving people are usually more responsive to sharing intimately than angry, upset people.

> A friend who was going through a painful divorce from his wife of thirty years had announced that he didn't want to talk about it with anyone. However, when I (Don) asked him to have lunch, it was only a matter of minutes before he freely began sharing some of the pain he was experiencing.

While not pushing my friend to share, I did intrude slightly into his intimate psychological zone by saying that I was sorry to hear about his divorce and if there was anything I could do to be helpful, I wanted him to know I was there to help. By carefully reading people on Channels Two and Three, we can more naturally match our territorial position to their preferences. It is through their manner and their body language that upset people say "come on in" or "back off."

Symbolic Communication

We have a powerful opportunity to provide comfort and consolation on *Channel Five*, the symbolic communication channel. It is often the small symbolic gestures that smooth pain and mean a lot. Phone calls, notes or visits to the elderly, to those who are weeks or months beyond the death of a loved one or to the housebound mean a great deal. Bringing food to the house of mourning, writing down a phone number for an upset friend, driving an elderly person to an appointment all provide significant support.

All of our lives are busy. None of us can minister to everyone. But each of us has the time to make a few symbolic gestures to someone in need. If we can be selective and not take on more than we can comfortably handle, the opportunity to make an impact is available. Think in small but meaningful terms. We may be able to send a card, bake a pie or fix a leaky faucet for the friend in need, whereas writing a long letter, preparing a three-course dinner for a family of eight or remodeling the neighbor's kitchen would burden us beyond our resources. The goal is to be helpful, not an angry and resentful martyr. One value of symbolic communication is that it reminds us that more often it is the "thought that counts" not the magnitude of the gesture.

Feelings

As you observe people who are dealing with a loss, you may notice many different feelings being expressed on *Channel Six*. It is not unusual for there to be feelings of numbness— times when feelings are repressed. Relief and happiness may even be experienced.

> Not long ago a woman expressed to us a bewildering potpourri of feelings. It had been her habit to call her mother every Saturday morning. For several months after her mother's death, she would awaken on Saturdays feeling happy and anticipatory about talking to her mother. When the reality of her mother's death sunk in, she would plunge into the depths of depression.

Upset may be demonstrated in a variety of ways. Whatever the feelings of upset people and whatever the style they employ to express those feelings, it is important to give permission for the person to have the feelings. Whether it be screaming, sobbing, silence, quiet tears, nervous laughter or constant chattering, we only need let it be. People have individual ways of expressing their feelings and their own time schedules for this release.

As for what you do with your own feelings during these times, we offer several suggestions. Very upset people often need the reassurance that someone is in control. Therefore, when possible, try to convey quiet strength and control. There are times, of course, when this is neither possible nor necessary. Our feelings may be intimately affected by our own involvement with the loss. When our closest friends are upset because they have just learned that the family will be moving across the country, we are also upset. Their move is our loss, too. In this case it is expected and appropriate to grieve together. But if a friend's mother whom we barely knew dies, our own feelings are not significantly involved. We can honestly turn most of our attention toward caring for our grieving friend. Try to match your emotional tone to the requirements of the situation. Your personal feelings of inadequacy and vulnerability mentioned at the beginning of this chapter are natural, but may need to be monitored. While it can be perfectly appropriate to say "I feel so inadequate at a time like this," it is not appropriate to *maintain* the spotlight on your own feelings. You may also find that you have to monitor feelings of irritation with the upset person. You may feel that they are grieving too "long" or too "strong." If you cannot talk to yourself about your own feelings in a way that helps your attitudes and your behavior, it might be wise to back away from the situation for a time.

Behavior

As in any kind of upset, our behavior, *Channel Seven*, influences people who are experiencing a loss. It is what we do, in addition to what we say, that counts. Phone calls, visits, letters, cooking for a bereaved family, watching the child of a sick friend or providing a meal to the family in the midst of a financial crisis are more than symbolic gestures. They are intentional actions that count for a lot. Gestures don't need to be big ones. They should, however, fill a need for the person who is experiencing the loss. Behaviors that best help upset people are actions that are helpful without being intrusive. Putting ourselves in the other person's shoes assists in finding this delicate balance. Asking ourselves "What would I want and/or need if my spouse had just died?" or "What would I appreciate if I were elderly, handicapped and without family?" are the kinds of questions that result in appropriate behavior.

In summary, the seven channels of communication provide a framework for dealing with upset people who are coping with the pain of loss or unwanted change. Silence, appropriate verbal and nonverbal expression of understanding and sympathy and symbolic and tangible gestures of your caring are the keys to successful handling.

The Formula and Practice

The basic formula for dealing with upset people is as applicable to dealing with grief as it is to dealing with the upset generated by complaints and anger. *Listening, empathizing, clarifying, problem solving and closing* are each a part of the process. There are, however, some unique timing issues related to dealing with those in grief. Whereas we can hope to resolve complaining or angry upset quickly, this is not so when it comes to upset created by loss or unwanted change. Time truly is the healer. Therefore, each of us needs to be patient with the upset bereaved person. As always, remember to use your caring parent first and then, only if necessary, your rational adult. Apply the channels of communication to the formula as suggested. Be aware of the kind of loss the upset person is experiencing and where the person is in the grief process. We believe that if you put all of this to work, not only will the upset person benefit, but you, too, will find the difficult task of comforting those in pain less frightening.

Practice is, as always, helpful. In this case, however, we realize that it is a bit macabre to plan what you will say and do if some tragedy should befall someone you know. What you can do, however, is remember some tough spots in which you have found yourself in the past. Try to remember not only what you did at the time but what effect it had on the upset people. Then, replay some of those experiences, imagining yourself using the suggestions presented in this chapter. In the future, when you have to deal with a difficult loss situation, allow yourself a few moments to review this chapter. When time permits, rehearse in your head what you might say and do. Be sure to remind yourself that, for the most part, little is expected from you. If you truly care, all you have to do is be there and let it show.

And Finally . . .

Before closing this chapter, there are four final suggestions we'd like to make. The first of these relates to the use of humor in dealing with upset people. Upset, particularly the upset generated by loss and bereavement, can make us "deadly" serious. Sometimes, a lighter touch is needed to relieve the tension. The value of humor was observed when we attended a friend's funeral last year. After the service, as friends and family were gathered together, laughter reverberated amid much reminiscing and joking. Suddenly, one of the guests said, "This is awful. Here we are laughing and carrying on at a funeral." Another guest offered, "I think this is great. No one liked a good party more than Fred did. In case you can hear us, Fred, this joke's for you."

Our second suggestion is don't overprotect the bereaved. For example, the couple who has lost a baby does not need to be protected from all talk of babies. If their friends who have babies avoid them, they are not protecting them but are in fact punishing them by withholding much needed support. It is artificial and uncomfortable for normal conversations to cease. The bereaved need support and comfort. They do not need for us to walk on eggshells. We'd like to underline at this point that if you feel in over your head, referral can be an excellent option. Referral may be helpful in providing distance from upset in which you are too emotionally involved. A good referral implies helpfulness. You are suggesting that there may be someone who can help the upset person better than you can. Referral is not failure. It is good common sense.

Finally, keep in mind that grieving people also can be needy people who unintentionally deplete our reserves. We need to take care of ourselves while caring for others. It is not surprising that many ministers, physicians, nurses, teachers and other helping professionals find their way into our counseling offices. Often, the problem is one of exhaustion — physical and emotional. The demands of other people can lead to fatigue. It is wise to know your limits; selectively choose when and where to help; and at times assertively say "no." All of our resources are finite. When we are emotionally drained, we cannot be helpful to anyone. This is a reminder to nourish and care for yourself while you are caring for others.

■

CHAPTER TEN
PUTTING IT ALL TOGETHER

TEN

He might have been considered a "young" manager in terms of his age and the number of years he had headed a department. But the members of his department saw him as a man of wisdom and compassion far beyond his years. Almost to a person, his workforce respected him. When queried as to the secret of his success in a role that frequently brings criticism, one departmental employee replied: "He is real, not a phony; usually pleasant and good natured. He tries to get to know us. He listens and he understands. He never seems to judge us. He rarely lectures us although he does provide the training and supervision we need we feel valued and appreciated. If we're upset he listens and if there's a problem he works with us until it's solved."

This story about a manager in a growing corporation illustrates beautifully what dealing with people is all about. The ideas discussed in this book are anchored in good old-fashioned common sense. None of the principles, formulas or strategies for handling upset people is very complicated. Yet, at times all of us find dealing with upset people a challenging task.

We began Chapter One by asking you to take the Dealing With Upset People Profile. Before reading any further, we would ask you to review the Profile found on pages six and seven, retaking it if you wish.

Of course, by now you know that the responses to the statements which lead to the best handling of upset people are numbers four and five. The Profile was not designed to be complicated or tricky but rather to reinforce attitudes and behaviors that will be useful to you as you find yourself confronted with people upset over a variety of issues and problems. Each statement on the Profile addresses an important point related to dealing with upset people. All of these concepts have been discussed in the book.

At this time we would like to restate the items on the Profile in a manner that highlights and summarizes the basic principles for *Dealing With Upset Persons.*

1) *Listen.* Good listening skills are the single most important tool for dealing with people who are upset. Being able to air feelings has prevented or cured a world of upset.

> Some years ago when my (Pennie's) son was on the threshold of young adulthood, he called from college with a moderate degree of upset over some career decisions that he needed to make. Like all parents, I had some ideas and opinions about his situation. Biting my tongue, I chose instead to say, "I'm not going to give you any advice. I love you very much and will support you in whatever decision you make. Can you share some of your own thinking as it pertains to this decision?" Not to my surprise, he proceeded to talk about his career concerns in a way that indicated he was aware of those issues that I wanted to be sure he was examining. He and I shared many of the same ideas and opinions, worries, fears and hopes. In his

process of "talking it out," he began to see more clearly which path to take. My role needed to be only one of being an "ear." Had I talked rather than listened, the decisions would have seemed to be more mine than his.

2) *Empathize.* There are two critical points to reiterate here. The first is a reminder of the importance of empathy — of being able to put oneself in another's shoes. Empathy, like listening, is an invaluable aid for defusing upset. The second is remembering that to understand is not to take responsibility. You can show concern and understanding without assuming liability. There is no need to hold back our understanding out of the fear of becoming responsible.

3) *Set the tone.* In our conversations with others, we have some responsibility for setting a tone or mood that is positive. If we let others set the tone, we are giving them too much power and control over us. Positive contact is critical to the prevention of upset. We will experience greater success in our relationships with others if the tone we set is a positive one.

4) *Caring parents and adults.* Calming upset people requires two basic behaviors from us: caring and rationality. We comfort upset people by behaving as caring parents. If the upset person has a problem that needs solving, we then use our rational adult. The critical person who convinces, lectures or moralizes is *not* successful with upset people.

5) *Focus your attention on others—particularly when they are*

upset. Most people prefer to talk about themselves than to listen to others, especially when they are upset. That's why listening is such a valuable skill. Good listeners allow others to talk. It is impossible to listen well while talking.

6) *People require attention.* Positive contact involves attending to others in a timely fashion. This avoids the secondary upset that results when people feel ignored. If people are already upset, having to wait for our attention adds to the strength of their upset feelings.

7) *You are not expected to have all the answers.* Being helpful doesn't mean having solutions or being a smooth talker.

8) *Upset people need to share their upset.* There is a strong need to air negative feelings when people are upset. The ventilation of upset is similar to the steam release valve on a pressure cooker. The release of steam prevents the cooker from exploding. Upset people may feel as if they are going to explode unless they can release some of their feelings. Therefore, whether or not there are solutions to reduce the upsetting problem and whether or not we can be helpful in finding that solution, we can help upset people just by listening to the expression of the upset.

9) *Listen nondefensively for issues.* We need to avoid the natural tendency to defend ourselves when attacked by upset people. The best way not to feel personally attacked is to listen for the *issues* in the person's upset rather than to focus on those comments which appear

to be blaming of us. If we can successfully focus our attention on the problem underlying the upset, we can help the other person to do likewise. And, if we can stay clear from feeling personally attacked, we are more likely to be able to maintain the helpful stances of a caring parent and a rational adult.

10) *Maintaining the goal of helpfulness.* The primary goal in dealing with upset people is to reduce their upset; to help them to feel better. Helping others to feel better also helps us. It is valuable if all the parties to an upsetting situation can maintain their self-esteem.

11) *The art of good referral.* A good referral is a sign of success. When the upset person needs something we cannot provide, a referral is not a sign of failure.

12) *People are responsible for themselves.* We are not always able to help someone who is upset. Some upset people choose to maintain an angry, critical, complaining or depressed stance. We can only do our best. We can't make people happy. Some problems can't be solved. All we can offer the upset person is a good ear and lots of understanding.

Some Parting Ideas . . .

Before we end our book, we'd like to leave you on a more philosophical note. We know that dealing with upset can be a trying and painful process. Negative emotions are difficult to handle. Many of us were never taught any skills for handling either our own negative emotions or those of other people. Take a few moments to think about the ways in which it was permissible for you to be angry as a child. We have asked this question of many people over the years. A majority of those to whom we have posed this question realized that all behaviors related to being angry or upset were criticized and thwarted. One man said, "Come to think of it, I wasn't allowed to yell; I wasn't allowed to be silent; I wasn't supposed to pout; I wasn't to say things that weren't nice; I wasn't allowed to slam doors or stomp around; I wasn't allowed to be physically angry in any way; I wasn't supposed to cry; and I wasn't allowed to have a tantrum. I guess when I think about it, I just wasn't ever supposed to be angry."

Most of us learned as children to be careful not to say or do anything that would anger other people. The childhood fear of upsetting others makes sense when we realize how dependent children are on other people to get their needs met. It can be very scary to feel helpless and to fear that the people you need may refuse to help you if they are angry at you. As we mature and develop, however, we become less helpless. We become responsible for taking care of ourselves. We no longer have to be quite so frightened that upsetting others will have dire consequences for us. And yet, these old childhood fears remain.

> Recently, we received a call from a woman named Elinor who was quite upset. She had just learned about a genetic problem in her family; a problem that might have serious implications for as yet unborn children in the family. Elinor's daughter and son-in-law were beginning to think about having a family. She had wanted to tell them about the implications for them of the

genetic problem but her husband had told her not to say anything. Elinor felt that it would not be "right" to stay silent. When asked what was keeping her from discussing the problem with her children, Elinor said, "I won't be able to live with myself if I don't tell my children about this, but I can't because my husband will be mad at me." After listening to Elinor's concerns, one of us asked with some intentional humor: "Will this be the first time your husband has ever been mad at you?" Elinor threw her head back and enjoyed a good laugh. "You've got a point there," she finally said. "I think I will have to do what *I* think is right. After all, it's me who has to live with me."

Elinor was responding as many of us do out of a mistaken idea that something catastrophic will happen if someone is upset with us. Anger, sadness, frustration and despair do not forecast catastrophe. They are just human emotions. As adults, we need to develop some comfort with the ability to handle the full range of emotions in ourselves and others. It is our strong belief that while "sticks and stones may break our bones," upset feelings do not have to hurt us. This belief encouraged us to develop and teach our seminar and to write this book.

Not only isn't the expression of upset harmful, but it can have great value. We mentioned earlier in the book that people who complain and share their upset are providing necessary feedback. We have to know what's upsetting someone before we can work on the problem. People who are willing to share their upset are trying to stay involved with us. In our experience as both family counselors and as business consultants we have learned that those least likely to resolve problems are those who are so resigned to failure that they have stopped talking and stopped fighting. To be upset, angry and sad is to care enough to share feelings and to care enough to put energy into trying to change things.

The expression of upset feelings can clear the air. People can feel better after an explosion of upset; be it through crying, yelling, slamming a door or taking a brisk walk. We need to remind ourselves that the expression of upset siphons off the steam.

While our primary goal is to prevent *unnecessary* upset in others through positive contact, some upset is necessary and/or inevitable. Consequently we have two important tasks to consider when dealing with those who are upset.

- how to handle our own feelings effectively
- how to deal with the upset person effectively

This book provides the formulas to assist you in these tasks. Let's quickly review the general formula for dealing with upset persons.

- Listen
- Empathize
- Clarify (Is there a problem? What is it?)
- Problem solve (if necessary)
- Close

The attitudes, behaviors and principles discussed throughout this book will help you exchange your old anxious feelings for concrete skills for dealing with upset people. We are convinced that the more you develop an optimistic attitude about complaints and upset and the more you practice the behaviors we have described, the better you'll get at handling upset people. If your life is a typical one, you will no doubt have numerous opportunities to put our suggestions to work. There will always be upset people. You now have the knowledge both to prevent unnecessary upset and to deal with those who are already upset. We wish you success! You and those whom your life touches will be the beneficiaries.

■

REFERENCES AND READINGS

Berne, E. (1967). *Games people play.* New York: Grove Press.

Bernstein, L., Bernstein, A.S., & Dana, R. (1974). *Interviewing: A guide for health professionals.* New York: Appleton-Century-Crofts.

Carkhuff, R.R. (1969). *Helping and human relations.* New York: Holt, Rinehart & Winston, Inc.

Ellis, A. & Grieger, R. (1977). *RET Handbook of rational-emotive therapy.* New York: Springer Publishing Co.

Guaspari, J. (1988). *The customer connection.* New York: AMACOM.

Harris, T. A. (1967). *I'm O.K.—You're O.K.* New York: Harper and Row.

Kübler-Ross, E. (1975). *Death the final stage of growth.* Englewood Cliffs, N.J.: Prentice-Hall.

Kübler-Ross, E. (1969). *On death and dying.* New York: Macmillan Publishing Co., Inc.

Lerner, H.G. (1985). *The dance of anger.* New York: Harper and Row

Maddux, R.B. (1988). *Successful negotiation.* Los Altos, California: Crisp Publications, Inc.

Peters, T. & Austin N. (1989). *A passion for excellence.* New York: Warner Books.

Peters, T. & Waterman, R.H.,Jr. (1988). *In search of excellence.* New York: Warner Books.

Puryear, D. A. (1979). *Helping people in crisis.* San Francisco: Jossey-Bass Publishers.

Satir, V. (1972). *Peoplemaking.* Palo Alto, California: Science and Behavior Books, Inc.

Silverstone, B., & Hyman, H.(1976). *You and your aging parents.* New York: Pantheon.

Staudacher, C. (1987). *Beyond grief: A guide for recovering from the death of a loved one.* Oakland, California: Harbinger Publications Inc.

Tavris, C. (1989). *Anger: The misunderstood emotion.* New York: Touchstone.

Villerè, M. F. (1981). *Transactional analysis at work.* Englewood Cliffs, N.J.: Prentice-Hall.

Wassmer, A. (1990). *Making contact: A guide to overcoming shyness.* New York: Henry Holt and Company.

Watzlawick, P., Weakland, J., & Fisch, R. (1974). *Change.* New York: W.W. Norton.

Zimbardo, P. (1977). *Shyness.* Reading, Mass: Addison-Wesley Publishing Co.

INDEX

About the Authors:

Pennie Myers Ed.D. is Marriage and Family Services Director and a member of the Gerontology faculty at The Wichita State University. Trained in counseling and a clinical member and approved supervisor for the American Association for Marriage and Family Therapy, Myers has expanded her family systems orientation into working with larger groups in business, industry and the professional community.

Don Nance, Ph.D. is Director of Counseling at The Wichita State University. Through his counseling, teaching and consulting, Nance has over twenty-five years experience working with people in a broad range of settings to manage a variety of problems. His ability to translate complex psychological principles into everyday language resulted in his being awarded his university's "Excellence In Teaching" award.

Myers and Nance have been a successful professional team for over fifteen years. In addition to their faculty positions, they are partners in Mid-America Consulting Services through which they have worked with a variety of clients including: health care organizations; church groups and volunteer organizations; school districts and local governments; small companies and large corporations. If you have an interest in presenting a program on Dealing With Upset People or providing other effective communication training, contact the authors, at The Wichita State University, Wichita, Kansas, 67208-1595, (316) 689-3440 or through Mid America Consulting (316) 689-4225.

ORDER FORM
Copy, Complete and Mail

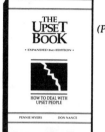

$12.⁹⁵
(Prices subject to change)

Please send _____ copies of **The Upset Book.**

Return order form to: **Mid America Services** **The Omni Center** **121 Whittier** **Wichita, KS 67207**	SHIPPING & HANDLING $2.00 for first book $1.00 each additional book Kansas residents add 5% tax.

Mailing Information:

Name _____

Position _____

Institution _____

Address _____

City _____ State _____ Zip _____

Phone_____

Method of Payment:

_____ Check enclosed   _____ P.O.# _____

_____ Visa   _____ Mastercard

Credit Card # _____

Expiration _____

Signature_____